PRAISE FOR *UNLOCKI*

"This is the approach for the 21st-century workplace. This informative and practical book shows how science can help us create flourishing organizations and flourishing people."
Vanessa King, Action for Happiness and author of *10 Keys to Happier Living*

"We all deserve to be happy at work. Jennifer Moss's ability to distil proven research into practical advice will help more of us get there."
Sarah Green Carmichael, Bloomberg opinion columnist and editor, former executive editor of *Harvard Business Review*

"*Unlocking Happiness at Work* is packed with provocative research and compelling examples of how to build higher performing individuals and teams. This book is a must-read for leaders of any organization seeking to become more innovative and elevate its performance."
Raj Sisodia, bestselling author of *Conscious Capitalism*, Co-Chairman, Conscious Capitalism Inc

"We know that happiness is a competitive advantage, but *Unlocking Happiness at Work* finally gives us the technical insight into how we can bring this science into our own organizations. Drawing on decades of hands-on experience, Jennifer Moss answers critical questions about the ways big and small data play a role in our happiness, whether technology can be a bridge or a barrier to well-being, and how the positive psychology movement has shaped our past, current and future state of happiness. A must-read for creating lasting culture change!"
Amy Blankson, bestselling author of *The Future of Happiness*

"Jennifer Moss leverages science, real-world examples and personal storytelling to detangle our misconceptions about the value of gratitude in our personal and professional lives. This book elegantly explains how gratitude can be taught and developed as the way to become our highest-performing selves."
Robert Emmons, Professor of Psychology at UC Davis and author of *Thanks!*

"Any business leader who wants to build higher-performing, innovative and compassionate teams should read this book. All of us know that great people make great companies. As a leader, I am always looking for better ways to engage our team, attract high-performing talent, disrupt and innovate while growing the current business. I understand that some may question the validity of a happiness strategy, but we can't ignore it any longer. Jennifer Moss uses scientific evidence and case studies to validate that authentic happiness at work will be the key to team member engagement for the most successful companies in 2030 and beyond. If you're like me and want to know how to stay ahead of the curve, you'll want to read her book."
Steve Carlisle, Former Executive Vice-President and President North America, General Motors

"Jennifer Moss gets it. *Unlocking Happiness at Work* is a no-fluff, research-backed call to action for leaders who are ready to ditch outdated playbooks and reimagine a workplace where people genuinely want to thrive. We need to go beyond where happiness isn't just a perk, but a core strategy, and leaders lead by example with authenticity and purpose. Read it, apply it, and watch what happens."
Jenn Lim, CEO of Delivering Happiness and bestselling author of *Beyond Happiness*

"In this intriguing, engaging and thoughtful narrative, Jennifer Moss takes a deeply personal and scientific dive into the secret of happiness in the workplace and beyond."
Emma Seppälä, PhD, Stanford Center for Compassion and Altruism Research and Education, Yale University Center for Emotional Intelligence

Unlocking Happiness at Work

How a Happiness Strategy Fuels Purpose, Passion and Performance

SECOND EDITION

Jennifer Moss

First published in Great Britain and the United States in 2016 by Kogan Page Limited
Second edition 2025

Kogan Page
Kogan Page Ltd, 2nd Floor, 45 Gee Street, London EC1V 3RS, United Kingdom
Kogan Page Inc, 8 W 38th Street, Suite 902, New York, NY 10018, USA
www.koganpage.com

EU Representative (GPSR)
Authorised Rep Compliance Ltd, Ground Floor, 71 Baggot Street Lower, Dublin D02 P593, Ireland
www.arccompliance.com

Kogan Page books are printed on paper from sustainable forests.

ISBNs
Hardback 9781398619494
Paperback 9781398619463
Ebook 9781398619470

British Library Cataloguing-in-Publication Data
A CIP record for this book is available from the British Library.

Library of Congress Control Number
2025933267

Typeset by Hong Kong FIVE Workshop
Print production managed by Jellyfish
Printed and bound by CPI Group (UK) Ltd, Croydon CR0 4YY

CONTENTS

FOREWORD

by Shawn Achor

Happiness researcher and New York Times *bestselling author of* Before Happiness

The world has changed.

In 2014 I was invited to speak at the Pentagon on the topic of positive psychology research. At the end of my presentation a senior warfare leader came up to me and said, 'Five years ago, the Pentagon could not have had a talk on happiness. Something has changed. Now we know that that conversation is crucial to organizational success.' This was a marked departure from when I started bringing positive psychology research from the labs at Harvard to companies. In 2006, at the beginning of the financial crisis, concepts of positive psychology seemed alien to senior leaders. Ten years later, nearly half of the Fortune 100 companies in 50 countries had invited me to work with them on happiness research. Many now realize that the greatest competitive advantage in the modern economy is a positive and engaged brain. The conversation truly has changed.

So why is the world ready for this message now? The first answer is actually the impetus for this book: having a quantitative approach to understanding the positive side of the curve has changed everything. For several decades, the world has known that subjective negative experiences like depression and trauma can be studied. But only recently has society, fuelled by the positive psychology movement, understood that happiness, gratitude and meaning are no different. Anything we can observe, we can quantify and then impact.

Jennifer Moss has been one of the biggest champions of this data-driven movement to study happiness using the tools of technology and big data. For several years, Jennifer, her husband Jim and I have been partners on projects that have looked for ways to connect leaders with the technologies and training that have helped not only move the needle, but change the calculus of positive leadership. Together Jennifer and I worked on a World Happiness Summit with Luis Gallardo, bringing together leaders from various levels of society – in business, education and health from Wall Street to

Bhutan – as we searched for ways to focus on a data-driven approach to happiness.

As Jennifer describes in this book, using data has allowed us to get past the mental or intellectual barriers that people can have. People who believe that happiness is soft are prejudiced. They have decided to hold fast to a belief that contradicts all the facts coming out of the scientific community which have shown how positive interventions have resulted in dramatic improvements to revenue, sales, energy, health, turnover and creativity in organizations. If happiness was left at the opinion level, both positive leaders and cynics would have to agree to disagree. But with the inclusion of scientific testing, we can now say to the cynics, 'You are incorrect.' Cynics can continue to doubt the importance of happiness, but they do so despite overwhelming data to the contrary.

The second reason for the change in the conversation is also well illuminated in this book. As self-described Gen Zs have now flooded into the job market, it has become abundantly clear that the old model of attracting and keeping talent is officially broken. In the past we assumed that increased hours and increased technology would automatically result in higher productivity and thus higher profitability. Think about the way that many law firms and hospitals are still run and you'll see the problem with this assumption. But now the most successful companies have turned the corner. They know that productivity and profitability drop if you increase hours, workload and stress. Only by creating positive social connections, training employees on optimism, revising our approach to stress and practising gratitude can we maximize the latent potential in our teams and families.

In this book, Jennifer Moss will describe the trajectory of change that is occurring and help you to find practical ways to own that change in your own life. We need you. We need more champions of positive research who will take the best practices that Jennifer outlines and bring them to their organizations and communities. If we continue this trend, we will find that we have exactly the type of organizations we seek: ones that maximize success without sacrificing meaning, connection or happiness. The world is changing – come with us.

Shawn Achor has become the leading expert on the connection between happiness and success. His research made the cover of Harvard Business Review, *his TED Talk is one of the most popular of all time with over 15 million views, and his HBO documentary on happiness in the NFL and two-hour interview with Oprah Winfrey have been seen by millions.*

Shawn spent 12 years at Harvard, where he graduated magna cum laude *and earned a Masters from Harvard Divinity School in Christian and Buddhist ethics. Shawn has now worked with nearly half of the Fortune 100 companies and with the White House, the Pentagon and NASA.*

Introduction

It has been nearly a decade since I completed the first manuscript for *Unlocking Happiness at Work*. A lot has changed since then. Including me.

Back then, I urged you to 'Choose happiness.' The reality is, choosing happiness isn't always that simple. And the idea that being happy is always in our control has put pressure on people to hide their unhappiness. Where the 'good vibes only' crowd are the only ones welcome.

Instead, let's choose happiness for others. Kindness gives us the same feel-good emotions associated with happiness but it's not the goal – it's a by-product of being kind.

What I've noticed in recent years is a slow eroding of altruism – defined as the 'unselfish regard for or devotion to the welfare of others'. An outcome of being told to avoid other humans at all cost – good for our physical safety – horrible for psychological safety. We'd play games of Pac-Man in grocery stores – deking in and out of aisles to avoid each other at all costs.

We've lived in a contradictory state for years. On one hand, our innate sense of self – the basis of humanity – is predicated on the fact that we need to cooperate to survive. On the other hand, we were warned that being in the same room with others – even our mothers and fathers – could put our survival at risk.

Years of social isolation has made it harder to make friends. Research that analysed astronauts involved in the Mars500 project, which simulated a long-duration mission to Mars, found that the confined and isolated environments led to interpersonal tensions, communication issues and psychological stress.[1]

Before, or as happiness expert, Jenn Lim and author of *Beyond Happiness*, likes to say, BC (Before Covid), we would tell a random stranger that we liked their shoes or buy someone a surprise coffee in the Starbucks line-up, but that's changed. A Forbes Health Study found that nearly 60 per cent of people say it's harder to make new friends as a result of the pandemic's impact.[2]

Novel research has concluded that this discomfort with connection is a result of widespread social anxiety – with an estimated additional 76.2 million cases of anxiety disorders globally, an increase of 25.6 per cent. Researchers determined that, 'It is unlikely that mental health will recover to pre-pandemic levels for some time.'[3]

Like a muscle that has atrophied, we need to exercise our conscience caring. We need to get kindness back into shape.

In the world of work, that lack of kindness is leading to a deep polarization between leaders and employees, generations struggling to find common ground and a labour force that feels left behind.

What's behind this shift? Over the past few years, we've become more transactional in our interactions, with tasks, deadlines and goals often prioritized over human connection.

But choosing kindness to unlock happiness at work goes a long way. A study published in the *Journal of Occupational Health Psychology* found that employees who engaged in acts of kindness experienced a 9 per cent increase in overall life satisfaction and a 6 per cent increase in job satisfaction in just four weeks.[4] These are not small numbers, especially as Gallup data shows engagement is continuing to fall at high rates.[5]

But today, in our hyper-competitive, efficiency-driven world, altruism – the selfless care for others – often feels like a luxury we can't afford. The irony is that we can't afford not to prioritize it. Altruism doesn't just benefit those on the receiving end – it provides significant happiness dividends to those who give as well. In one experiment published in *The Journal of Social Psychology*, employees who engaged in prosocial behaviour reported feeling more positive emotions and satisfaction with their work than those who didn't.[6]

And the benefits don't stop there. When companies build a culture of altruism and kindness, they see the ripple effects in their bottom line. Research published in the *Harvard Business Review* highlights the significant impact of trust on workplace performance. The study found that employees in high-trust organizations reported 74 per cent less stress, 106 per cent more energy at work, 50 per cent higher productivity, 13 per cent fewer sick days, 76 per cent more engagement and 40 per cent less burnout compared to those in low-trust environments.[7]

So, how do we reclaim kindness? It starts with us. Leaders must model the behaviours so employees can spread the contagion. It's all about simple acts of support, recognition and acknowledgement. Bringing back the 'thank you's' we've forgotten because we've been too busy. Celebrating good ideas and calling out good people.

It also means going back to the fundamentals of what makes us human. The solutions are simpler than we think, and sometimes simple solutions are the ones that scare us the most. Because they are possible. Now we're 'on the hook' for positive change.

Ten years later and here we are – in an even more divided and disconnected world. When I wrote the first edition, I was optimistic that we were heading for positive change. Today, more than ever, we need to get back to basics. We need to focus on what is both familiar and novel – like a 'Golden Rules Strategy'. Where our happiness at work plan is rooted in key messages of kindness, empathy and self-compassion. The kinds of things our grandma would say.

What if we could rekindle some of the favourites? Like, 'Honesty is the best policy' to counter the crisis of disinformation. 'Patience is a virtue' to curb our addiction to immediate gratification. We'd say 'Water under the bridge' instead of 'cancel culture'. An overworked and burned-out workforce could benefit from, 'You can't pour from an empty cup.' And, as we watch our political leaders hit lower and lower, we'd remind them, 'Two wrongs don't make a right.'

As we look to rebuild trust and unlock happiness at work with our people and teams, bringing back the basics is the only way forward. To break free of this unhealthy and unhappy trap we're in – where work feels like a grind – let's make it our mission to make it a bit happier for someone else. As my grandma would say, 'A little kindness goes a long way.'

Notes

1 Y Wang, X Jing, K Lv, B Wu, Y Bai et al During the long way to Mars: Effects of 520 days of confinement (Mars500) on the assessment of affective stimuli and stage alteration in mood and plasma hormone levels, *PLOS ONE*, 2014 9 (4), e87087. doi.org/10.1371/journal.pone.0087087 (archived at https://perma.cc/DAC6-U2B9)

2 S Davis. 59% of US adults find it harder to form relationships since covid-19, survey reveals – here's how that can harm your health, Forbes, 2022. www.forbes.com/health/mind/social-anxiety-since-covid-survey (archived at https://perma.cc/9AKF-947N)

3 R Kindred and G Bates. The influence of the Covid-19 pandemic on social anxiety: A systematic review, *International Journal of Environmental Research and Public Health*, 2023. pmc.ncbi.nlm.nih.gov/articles/PMC9915904 (archived at https://perma.cc/V2FX-4JQG)
4 www.apa.org/pubs/journals/ocp (archived at https://perma.cc/A63K-VBLH)
5 J Harter. US employee engagement inches up slightly after 11-year low, Gallup, 2024. www.gallup.com/workplace/647564/employee-engagement-inches-slightly-year-low.aspx (archived at https://perma.cc/X823-HX77)
6 *The Journal of Social Psychology*
7 P Zak. The neuroscience of trust, *Harvard Business Review*, 2017. hbr.org/2017/01/the-neuroscience-of-trust (archived at https://perma.cc/8LHN-DWTJ)

1

The happiness/ brain science connection

After years of observing the highest-performing workplace cultures, I've come to recognize that these firms share three key traits.

They demonstrate high emotional intelligence – the ability to understand and navigate emotions in themselves and others. They provide psychological safety – people feel free to express ideas and take risks without fear of judgement or retribution. Finally, they have extraordinary trust – not just in leadership but with each other.

All of this combined makes up the most psychologically fit organizations. Failure is learning. Feedback is welcome. Curiosity is encouraged. Respectful communication is a requirement. Work is challenging – it can also be fun.

Just as a brain that is healthy and happy is high-performing, so is an organization. Brains that continually confront harmful toxins have to shut down in order to prevent any more threats. This is also what happens inside toxic organizations with weak cultures.

We only need to look at a brain under stress to imagine what a firm under stress looks like. Despite fears that artificial intelligence (AI) will take over our jobs, I predict that there is no world in which humans aren't part of the workforce. It's in our genetic coding to evolve. It's how we keep our species alive. Mass unemployment is also terrible for the global economy.

So, to understand happiness at work we need to understand happiness at the individual level. What motivates people and what holds them back? What drives innovation and the ability to get our workforce ready for the future? To be at their best, our people need a clear and healthy mind to solve big problems. A well workforce is no longer a 'nice to have' – it's a necessity.

As leaders, we will encounter difficult decisions every day. We will be asked to remain neutral but empathetic, risk-taking but steady, immovable but malleable. Our brains require the highest level of psychological fitness to master these decisions and yet be able to bounce back when we've taken a step in the wrong direction.

It's vital to understand that well-being must be impacted upstream. I wrote in my 2021 book *The Burnout Epidemic* that we can't solve chronic stress and burnout with self-care alone. The World Health Organization (WHO) has identified burnout as workplace and/or institutional stress left unmanaged.

Burnout is a pervasive problem that goes beyond individual stress – it is an organizational issue rather than just a personal one.

Burnout is defined by three primary characteristics: exhaustion, cynicism and a sense of ineffectiveness – and it is driven by systemic factors like unmanageable workloads, lack of control, insufficient rewards for effort, lack of community, unfairness and value conflicts in the workplace. Solving burnout requires addressing these root causes rather than expecting individuals to cope better through self-care or resilience-building alone. The solution must come from leaders rethinking workplace culture and policies to foster sustainable, healthy environments.

It takes time to develop a habit of healthiness in our personal lives, so we need to imagine it will take time to build a great culture focused on wellness. Far too often, leaders want to lean on 'silver bullet' solutions like apps and looking back surveys for their well-being programming. But the most successful strategies are based on simple principles: patience, commitment and time. In a world that is moving at breakneck speed that simple strategy can feel impossible. We must remember that anything worth having requires hard work.

We'll get into how we can prevent stress in later chapters, but first let's start by examining the concepts of positive psychology – the scientific study of strengths and virtues that enable individuals and communities to thrive, focusing on enhancing well-being and fostering resilience.

Training the brain for happiness and high-performance

A hand grasps a fork and digs into the apple pie and ice cream on the plate. It scoops up an oversized bite and brings it towards the mouth where it will soon be chewed and swallowed. But before any of this physical activity occurs, our brain and body are already hard at work.

As soon as we see or smell the food, sensory cues activate our brain's limbic system, which governs emotion, memory and hunger. This leads to a surge of saliva and digestive enzymes as we prepare to indulge. Meanwhile, the hormone ghrelin is released, increasing our appetite and signalling the body that food is on the way. Our brain's reward centre also triggers the release of dopamine, creating a sense of excitement even before we take the first bite.[1]

The moment food hits our taste buds, the pleasure response intensifies. Different flavours – sweet, salty, sour, bitter and umami – send signals to the brain, reinforcing the enjoyment. Dopamine surges again, solidifying the association between eating and happiness. As the food reaches the stomach, digestive hormones work together to signal satisfaction and fullness. The combination of sensory pleasure, dopamine-driven reward and a well-coordinated digestive response makes eating a delicious meal a powerful experience that enhances our happiness and well-being.[2]

It's believed that the brain processes around 11 million bits of information per second. However, of those, only about 40 to 50 bits are consciously attended to, leaving the rest to be handled subconsciously.[3]

Eating is an example of where our conscious and subconscious brain activities collide to help us live more effectively and efficiently. If we had to attend to all of the things running in the background, we would be overwhelmed. Imagine you had to tell your body which hormones need to be released to process your food. Imagine if you had to remember to take each and every breath.

The same applies to emotions. Just like the chemical processes that are triggered by hunger, emotions are also complex sets of chemical data that travel via our neural pathways from one part of our brain to another. Each node sets off different signals depending on the chemical compound. Joy (or sadness), like hunger, is just one compound of many that make up the emotional ecosystem inside our brains.

The field of neurosciences, specifically social neuroscience, has been recognized for expanding traditional psychology by examining how brain structures influence our social behaviours. It also helps us to understand the way happiness occurs in the brain and subsequently how to translate that brain activity into personal and professional performance. Ground-breaking research in the field of neural and psychological sciences can teach us how to strengthen our psychological fitness so we can be higher-performing.

Let's get started at the centre of it all – the neural pathways that are rapidly wiring and rewiring our behaviours to leverage the habits of happiness inside our brains.

Neural pathways and behaviour

For centuries, psychologists have studied how the mind interplays with the physical architecture of the brain. New research has provided groundbreaking insights into the brain–body connection, revealing just how deeply intertwined our physical and mental states are.

One fascinating discovery, published by researchers from Washington University, identified a previously unknown brain network called the somato-cognitive action network (SCAN). This network links parts of the brain responsible for movement to regions involved in thinking, planning and controlling vital bodily functions, such as heart rate and blood pressure. It challenges the traditional view that motor functions are separate from cognitive processes, showing how movement, goal setting and physiological regulation are interconnected. This network helps explain how our body reacts to stress, thoughts and emotions, supporting the idea that the brain is wired to maintain harmony between physical actions and mental states.[4]

Studies on the vagus nerve, which connects the brainstem to the body, highlight its crucial role in mediating the brain–body connection. The vagus nerve influences everything from emotional regulation to digestive processes. Research has shown that stimulating this nerve can have profound effects on mood and stress responses, opening new possibilities for treating anxiety and depression. This connection between interoception (the body's ability to sense its internal state) and emotions further solidifies the emerging understanding that our mental well-being is deeply rooted in how the brain communicates with the body.[5]

A growing group of scientists believe that this mind–body connection can be explained through the way our body and mind talk to one another. Hormones travel throughout the body and signal various emotional responses, using the endocrine system as the conversation channel of choice. To back up slightly for any of you unfamiliar with how the above works, the endocrine system is a collection of glands that produce hormones to regulate metabolism, growth and development, tissue function, sexual function, reproduction, sleep and mood, among other things. In addition to the nervous system, the endocrine system is a major communication system of the body. While the nervous system uses neurotransmitters as its chemical signals, the endocrine system uses hormones.[6]

So how does this translate into body and brain collaborations as it relates to our moods and subsequent happiness?

For starters, hormones like testosterone can increase assertiveness, confidence and competitiveness. Adrenaline can induce both fear and excitement. Cortisol increases our chance of survival from imminent threat, but can also depress us both physically and emotionally.

Kelly McGonigal, bestselling author and Stanford professor, notes in her book, *The Willpower Instinct*, 'The gut has its own neurotransmitters that are the physiological basis for intuition and gut feelings. Even the immune system can commandeer our mind by reacting to stress through our moods and our bodies simultaneously.'[7]

'Rich psychological experiences may be rooted in the body,' says McGonigal. 'It doesn't make falling in love less meaningful, art less creative, or the mind less fascinating… working from this premise, we can understand puzzles like why loneliness increases your risk of heart disease, or how brain injuries transform personalities… or why working out improves memory.'[8]

To help us to better understand how the mind and the brain actually work in a complementary and interdependent relationship, we have to look deeper into the complex study of neuroscience.

The term 'neuroplasticity' is derived from the root words 'neuron' and 'plastic', and refers to the brain's ability to reorganize by creating new neural pathways to adapt, as it needs. Neuroplasticity refers to our brains' ability to be malleable, or plastic, so that our experiences can change both the brain's physical structure (anatomy) and functional organization (physiology).[9]

After a brief background on how psychological sciences and neurosciences bumped into each other, we'll look deeper into how our brain's plasticity assists us in building habits, inspires our actions, changes our negative behaviours and fights boredom. There are numerous ways to unlock happiness, and it all starts by optimizing the brain to improve the mind.

The history of neuroplasticity

It was in 1890 that William James first suggested the existence of neuroplasticity. In his book *The Principles of Psychology*[10] he proposed that the human brain is capable of reorganizing. Although James was amongst the first to suggest that the brain could be altered by our behaviours, the term 'neuronal plasticity' was coined by Santiago Ramón y Cajal (1852–1934). The term started a controversial discussion between scientists who still believed that we have a fixed number of neurons in our adult brains that cannot be replaced when cells die.

The idea of cellular death remains hotly debated. None of us wants to think that one too many days without sleep will kill off our precious brain cells – permanently. It isn't like we don't get enough of these prized neurons at birth. In the early years of life, humans manufacture an estimated 250,000 neurons per minute, and then spend the next few years wiring them together.[11] So, you'd think we had enough to work with.

What is important to know about neurogenesis (cellular reproduction) is that we don't need new neurons to change our brain. Obviously, we'd like to think more neurons mean more intelligence, but that isn't exactly the case. Instead, we're better to focus on the wiring, or even rewiring, of those neurons that are ready and waiting to be plugged into.

Neuroplasticity also plays a key role in unlocking self-awareness and, subsequently, personal growth. Our brains crave novelty through exposure to new and novel experiences. It explains how we can build a jogging habit after years of sedentary living, or be capable of adapting to a life in a big city after growing up in a small town. It helps some of us rebuild hope after tragedy, or have empathy for people we've never met.

The list goes on.

But, what does this all mean for us at work and at home, in our lives and our ability to perform and be happy?

A lot.

Neuroplasticity is the brain's ability to change and adapt over time. So, even if we've developed certain habits or ways of thinking, our brain can essentially rewire itself to create new patterns – which is why we can learn new skills, break bad habits or recover from brain injuries. Essentially, it's the brain's way of saying, 'I can grow and change.'

If we are able to imagine that positive habits can be built over time, we can also imagine a process of eliminating unhealthy habits for a happier life and a happier experience of work.

Breaking the hardwired habits

John Cacioppo, a pioneering social psychologist and neuroscientist at the University of Chicago, made significant contributions to understanding how the brain processes social experiences. Through his use of tools like electroencephalograms (EEG) and functional magnetic resonance imaging (fMRI), Cacioppo discovered that when people feel isolated or disconnected their brains respond in ways that increase cognitive and emotional stress, making them more susceptible to negative behaviours like aggression, defensiveness or withdrawal.[12]

This has important implications for workplace behaviour, because employees who feel socially isolated or excluded may not perform at their best, and their ability to collaborate or engage productively is diminished.

These insights have led to a better understanding of why social environments are so critical to workplace behaviour and the mental health of employees.

For leaders, the key takeaway is that while negative behaviours – like bias and bullying – may seem entrenched, they can be modified.

By understanding the brain's adaptability, leaders can foster environments that encourage the formation of prosocial behaviours such as empathy, cooperation and psychological safety. This shift doesn't happen overnight, but with commitment to new patterns, both individuals and teams can transform how they operate.

Rethinking bias

Over the years, social psychologists have found that the brain automatically, and in large part unconsciously, places people and objects into categories such as 'familiar' and 'foreign', 'good' and 'bad'. According to collaborative research between New York University and Yale, neuroscientists discovered that this categorization then biases people's feelings and reactions towards those people and things.[13] This topic can be considered controversial because it identifies that we have unique, built-in biases that are not just taught but coded in the brain. This encoding is thought to be a result of our brain becoming accustomed to familiar surroundings so it uses the same filter when looking at something new.

Our brains are especially active when we look at unfamiliar faces, and because humans tend to fear the unfamiliar this triggers stress inside the brain. As our workforce becomes increasingly global, it becomes paramount to use empathy as a means to combat our stereotyped responses. Using empathy while developing diverse teams, we are able to cognitively familiarize with another person's experience. And that familiarity allows our brain to settle in to a healthy balance of comfort and fluency. When our brain is content, it will move past its ingrained patterns and remain open.

To explain it in business outcomes, if our brains were more psychologically safe at work, we could ensure our frontline staff handled irate customers with less fear and improve the compatibility between employees and their managers. Imagine these were the tools in the emotional toolbox available to every person who worked for you. What would it mean if your people could pull out their 'resiliency hammer' or their 'empathy driver' whenever the task required it?

Similar to how we are nervous of trying new foods or of taking a risk because it is an unknown, we also shy away from making new connections due to these deeply embedded stereotypes. For example, it's now a common practice to review a candidates social media profiles or Google their background before an interview. This exercise has been challenged by diversity, equity, inclusion and accessibility (DEIA) advocates as exclusionary because of our hardwired bias. Today, DEIA experts suggest we remove screening processes that can leave out vulnerable applicants.

A study published in 2021 by the University of Chicago found that job applicants with 'Black-sounding' names were 50 per cent less likely to receive call-backs compared to those with 'white-sounding' names. The study emphasized that biases can be pervasive even when qualifications are identical.[14]

Another study involving law firms found that male candidates from higher-class backgrounds were more likely to benefit from their status, while women from similar backgrounds faced a 'commitment penalty', as they were perceived as less dedicated due to assumptions about family life.[15]

Additionally, AI tools designed to assist in recruitment often replicate these biases, as shown by studies where Black applicants received 30 per cent fewer call-backs compared to their white counterparts when using AI-driven platforms.[16]

It's crucial that we consciously address our own biases and develop more effective strategies to prevent these deeply ingrained, subconscious tendencies from excluding qualified talent. Even more critical is ensuring that the systems designed to be neutral don't unintentionally adopt our biases – because when we trust these systems to be impartial, they could perpetuate and even amplify the problem.

Attitudes

People are wired to seek social connections and belonging. Our attitudes towards people, products and brands are often connected to how they give us a sense of community or group identity. This psychological need for belonging reinforces certain attitudes. It makes us choose Coke over Pepsi. It also makes us choose one person over another to hire, promote and include.

A culture that has strong value alignment between their people and the mission helps to remove culture barriers and attitudes of exclusion. Instead, you get everyone working towards the same goal.

A study by Samuel McClure and colleagues proved how strongly held biases can heavily influence our decisions. He combined simple taste tests of Coke and Pepsi and event-related fMRI to probe the neural responses that correlate with the behavioural preferences for the two soft drinks.[17] A total of 67 subjects participated in the study. In the double-blind taste tests, the researchers found that subjects split equally in their preference for Coke and Pepsi in the absence of brand information. But when the drinks were explicitly labelled, Coke won the taste test by a landslide. New research has discovered that participants with pre-frontal cortex damage did not show a preference for either brand in both scenarios, which highlights how deep our affinity to brands can run.[18]

In the context of work, research suggests our brains react similarly towards leaders for which we have a positive affinity.

Several studies have found that when leaders embody characteristics that followers admire – such as empathy, clear vision or ethical behaviour – these traits activate similar neural circuits as seen in brand loyalty. Leaders who can articulate a vision that aligns with followers' goals and identity tap into the same neurological pathways that brands use to create emotional attachment.[19]

On the flipside, closed-minded attitudes can prevent us from inviting new ideas to a discussion. We might not bring someone in from a different department to a brainstorming session despite the benefits of receiving unfiltered feedback. Our prevailing attitudes might assume that a developer doesn't understand trends, or a marketer can't code.

We've seen this collective cliquing get in the way of higher thinking and problem solving, more so in recent years. A study by Harvard Business School Professor Tiona Zuzul analysed hundreds of billions of emails between workers at thousands of organizations globally between 2019 and

2020. The data revealed that 'employees were digitally splitting off into more isolated and well-defined communication networks'.[20]

As leaders, we need to force ourselves constantly to think laterally and vertically. If not, we will find our collective brains stuck in prescribed patterns, which hinders innovation and global competitiveness. It also makes our workplace less psychologically safe – counter to high-performing workplace cultures and employee happiness.

Self-control

Emotional regulation is a sign of a healthy mind. Conversely, one of the major symptoms of stress and burnout is emotional dysregulation. It's why we see more negative gossip and sniping in high-stress workplace environments. Someone who used to be fairly agreeable seems to be constantly oppositional or quick to anger. You may also notice that there are way bigger swings between the highs and lows.

For leaders and managers, emotional regulation is an essential skill. In times of high volatility and change, it's helpful to meet chaos with calm.

I want to be clear that emotional control is not being devoid of feelings. Actually, the reverse is true. Emotional leadership is the key to connecting on a personal level with those we lead.

A high level of emotional regulation also tells us in which situations to exhibit empathy, compassion and enthusiasm. It helps us to mirror another's moods to better engage and build rapport. Emotional control is about leveraging our emotions in a positive, healthy way.

Take these two leaders for examples: Elon Musk and Satya Nadella.

Elon Musk, CEO of X (formerly known as Twitter), is known for emotional outbursts and unpredictable behaviour. His 'funding secured' tweet about taking Tesla private led to a lawsuit and fines, destabilizing Tesla's stock and creating significant operational challenges.[21] Since Elon Musk took over Twitter in October 2022, the company has seen significant turnover and structural changes. It's estimated that over 6,000 employees have been laid off under Musk's leadership, which represents about 80 per cent of the company's workforce.

Additionally, X has faced challenges in user engagement and advertiser relationships. The platform has lost almost 50 per cent of its advertising revenue since the acquisition, causing further instability.

In terms of workforce stability, many key executives and senior leaders have resigned or were let go, which has further impacted morale and operations within the company. This high turnover rate and organizational uncertainty have contributed to ongoing concerns about the platform's future direction.

In contrast, Satya Nadella is often described as a calm and composed leader who excels in emotional regulation, which is a key aspect of his leadership style. Since taking over as CEO of Microsoft, he has been widely recognized for his ability to stay calm under pressure and lead with empathy, even in difficult situations.

Under his leadership, Microsoft's market value has soared by over $800 billion, and its stock price has more than quadrupled. Nadella focused on transforming Microsoft's hyper-competitive environment into one that fosters empathy, collaboration and a growth mindset.[22]

One of the first actions Nadella made when he took over from his predecessor Steve Ballmer was to remove the controversial 'stack ranking' system – a performance management method in which employees are ranked relative to each other, typically on a scale from best to worst. Under this system, managers must assign employees into fixed performance categories, often referred to as top, middle and bottom performers, based on their relative performance. The top performers are rewarded with bonuses or promotions, while the bottom performers face potential consequences such as demotion or termination.[23]

Nadella did away with a system that bred internal competition and stifled innovation, and replaced it with a culture that rewards teamwork and shared success. Employees are now encouraged to adopt a growth mindset, learning from failures and emphasizing continuous improvement, a change that has contributed to significant boosts in morale and productivity.

The key point here is that emotional regulation does not mean that we hide our emotions. We don't have to pretend that we're 'all good'; rather, we leverage our emotions to 'do good'. Essentially, we're practising altruism, which requires being considerate of others by taking pauses instead of acting on impulse, listening more than talking, showing compassion by actioning what we hear, and being honest without being brutal.

Reframing

Cognitive reframing is a psychological technique that consists of identifying and then challenging irrational thoughts. It offers a way of experiencing negatively interpreted events and emotions to find more positive alternatives. 'Reframing is about changing the meaning we give to events, not necessarily changing the events themselves.'[24]

Let's now examine a few scenarios where we could reframe our conversations at work:

> 'I tried that already' could become 'What can we do differently this time?'
> 'This has been an absolute failure' could become 'What did I learn?'
> 'I don't have any time' could become 'What can I stop doing that isn't a priority, to free up more time?'

We can also take reframing interventions into our communications with our people. We have all heard or made statements such as, 'If I only had X, I could do my job better,' or, 'If I only had X, I could accomplish my goal,' or, 'If I only had X, I would have a better relationship with my boss.' You get the picture. And yet, we can give individuals the tools to reframe their negative experiences at work. It requires shifting their mindset so they can identify opportunities where their workplace helps them to complete their project/achieve their goals/improve their relationships, rather than hinders them.

Reframing leverages simple yet powerful tools that all of us have access to – perspective and language. When we perceive our experiences as opportunities versus challenges, and then use the power of language to verbalize those perceptions, we develop more prosocial behaviours.

As a leader, this helps us to better inspire and engage the people we lead. When we allow negative events to fester, it can become an unhealthy contagion. Reframing helps us to shift attitudes and pull people out of a negative state.

The ever-adapting memory

We don't just carry old baggage with us from one bad breakup to the next new relationship. We also carry around old memories of horrible bosses, incompatible teammates and stressful workplaces. Memories are actually quite tricky. We tend to think of our memories as a kind of video recording, of which we can hit rewind and watch our past in a perfectly restored film. However, memories are nothing like that. Instead, memories rewrite the past with current and new information, updating our memory with new experiences.

Donna Jo Bridge, when she was a postdoctoral fellow at Northwestern University Feinberg School of Medicine, conducted research demonstrating that our memory is faulty because it actively rewrites the past. Her study showed that memories are not static, but instead are reshaped every time they are recalled. This means that each time we remember something, we might be unintentionally altering details based on our current experiences or feelings, leading to distorted or even false recollections. She explains that memories 'insert things from the present into memories of the past when those memories are retrieved'.[25]

A 2021 study from Imperial College London found that, while memories are consolidated, the brain selectively stabilizes only certain pieces of information, meaning we don't always retain complete or accurate details.[26]

The reason we do this? To help us survive.

We need to adapt to ever-changing environments, so mixing new knowledge with old knowledge helps us to deal with today's priority.

'Everyone likes to think of memory as this thing that lets us vividly remember our childhoods or what we did last week,' said Joel Voss, Assistant Professor of Medical Social Sciences and Neurology at Feinberg. 'But memory is designed to help us make good decisions in the moment and, therefore, memory has to stay up-to-date. The information that is relevant right now can overwrite what was there to begin with.'[27]

Reframing a memory is a powerful psychological tool that helps individuals manage stress and trauma by changing the emotional significance of the memory. In the workplace, where employees often face challenging situations that can leave lasting emotional imprints, developing this skill is particularly useful.

Conflict with co-workers, failure in a project, or being overlooked for a promotion can lead to persistent negative emotions that affect performance and workplace relationships. By reframing these memories, employees can shift their perspective and focus on what they learned from the experience, how they've grown, or how they can approach similar situations differently in the future.

This strategy leverages the brain's memory reconsolidation process, where, each time a memory is recalled, it becomes flexible and open to re-interpretation.[28] For example, an employee who feels slighted by a past failure can reframe the memory to see it as a stepping stone towards success or personal development.

As shown in cognitive behavioural therapy (CBT), reframing helps in altering the emotional impact of past events, turning negative memories into opportunities for growth rather than sources of distress. Leaders in the workplace can support this process by creating environments that encourage reflection, feedback and learning from setbacks, helping their teams rewire how they perceive challenging experiences.

How our brains fire and wire

As we investigate the laws of science as they relate to happiness, the best way to sum it up comes from Donald Hebb, a Canadian psychologist who famously stated, 'The neurons that fire together, wire together.'

Neuropsychologist Rick Hanson, author of *Hardwiring Happiness: The new brain science of contentment, calm, and confidence*, emphasizes that this process can be harnessed for personal growth, particularly in overcoming the brain's natural negativity bias. Our negative-leaning attitudes are remnants of an evolutionary hangover going as far back as our cave-dwelling days. This annoying carryover makes our brains act like Velcro to negative experiences and Teflon to positive ones. It has us irrationally scanning for sabre-tooth tigers on the prowl ready to attack us at any moment.[29]

This fear is deeply rooted in our subconscious and is still very much alive and well in our day-to-day lives. The subsequent chemical reaction to fear is often referred to as our 'fight or flight' response. And, when the chemistry is active, the part of our brain called the hippocampus region yanks itself offline to ensure its protection. Since the lower brain is responsible for creative and innovative thinking, a brain state in fight or flight can reduce as much as 30 per cent of that imaginative headspace, essential for new ideation.[30]

Hanson suggests that we can counteract this bias by consciously 'taking in the good' – savouring positive moments for at least 10–30 seconds to allow them to create lasting neural changes. He elaborates on how repeatedly focusing on positive experiences strengthens these neural pathways, turning fleeting moments of joy, gratitude or success into lasting psychological resources. By doing this, we can cultivate qualities like resilience, confidence and happiness, gradually reshaping our brain for the better through self-directed neuroplasticity.

The motivated brain

The ventral tegmental area (VTA) and the ventral striatum are two distinct regions of the brain that work together to identify whether the risk and the effort is worth the reward.

The VTA sends dopamine signals to several areas of the brain, and with that release comes feelings of pleasure, motivation and reward. It reinforces behaviours that may be considered pleasurable or beneficial, like eating, socializing and striving for goals.

The ventral striatum is involved in processing rewards and reinforcement. This area of the brain receives the dopamine signals from the VTA and helps translate those signals into action. Essentially, it's when our subconscious decides whether what we do next is worth the effort.[31]

It should come as no surprise, then, that boredom – labelled today as 'boreout'[32] in the workplace context – is a major driver of unhappiness at work. When employees face repetitive, monotonous work, the brain essentially powers down. Without activation of the reward system, motivation plummets. In this sense, the brain is like a muscle that requires varied, stimulating 'workouts' to stay engaged – essentially it craves novelty. When it doesn't get these workouts, it starts to atrophy in terms of motivation and enthusiasm.

Consider an employee who spends months doing nothing but routine data entry. At first, they might enjoy the predictability of the task, but, over time, the lack of challenge turns that initial ease into boredom. Their brain, no longer receiving hits of dopamine from new challenges or problem-solving, begins to disengage. This disengagement doesn't just affect the individual – it spreads through the team, dampening morale and productivity. Studies show that employees experiencing boreout often go to great lengths to appear busy, a behaviour that drains both their energy and the company's overall efficiency.[33] It's the workplace equivalent of 'faking it until you make it', except you never quite make it.

To mitigate the impacts of boreout, organizations must introduce novelty and variety into employees' work lives. One powerful intervention is job rotation or cross-functional projects, which can inject a sense of newness and activate the brain's reward centres.

Another effective strategy is incorporating more gamification into work processes – turning routine tasks into interactive, game-like experiences taps into the brain's natural desire for novelty and reward. Imagine how a sales team might be reinvigorated by turning weekly sales goals into a fun, points-based challenge, where progress triggers a dopamine release that keeps motivation high.

Ultimately, combating boreout is about creating a dynamic work environment where employees' brains are regularly fed with new tasks, challenges and opportunities for growth. In doing so, organizations can help reactivate the reward centres of their employees' brains, leading to greater engagement, creativity and well-being in the workplace.

Delivering meaning

So, the question now becomes, 'How do we combat boredom if repetition is an unavoidable aspect of the job?'

Some of us may be leading manufacturing teams, line workers or administrative assistants; roles that still require engagement but consist of repetitive work. Employees that engage in repetitive work and still feel very happy and satisfied tend to find more meaning in their roles – meaning that goes beyond the tasks they perform every day.

In the study 'How to motivate assembly line workers' at Jonkoping International Business School, manufacturing employees who identified as being the most engaged in their roles answered the following about why they liked their job:[34]

1. 'Otherwise the customer would not get clean products, the company would not have customers, and we would not have jobs.'
2. 'We provide clean textiles to hotels all over Sweden. If we do our job right, the hotel staff can do their job right = happy hotel customers.'

When an employee working on the line at a manufacturing plant believes that every time they pull out that faulty bolt or screw from the pile on the conveyor belt they could be saving a life, it can trigger a stronger sense of purpose and commitment to their work. They become part of the bigger picture and as a result tend to demonstrate higher levels of engagement.

In my book *Why Are We Here?* I discuss the importance of connecting purpose and meaning to work for higher engagement. In it I write about the power of storytelling.

Imagine the difference between an employee who knows and believes that their efforts are contributing to building a safer helmet or protective vest for a police officer versus someone who never knows the outcome of their efforts.

Who do you think would feel more fulfilled in what they do every day?

Often, the stories of how the end user is benefiting from the products we make are lost. Pulling people into the broader goals helps provide meaning to everyday jobs. We need to do a better job of bringing these stories back to our employees so they are connected to what they do every hour, every day.

As we can see from the literature, the brain's desire for stimulus is a creature that must be fed. Since boredom can't be erased entirely from our workplaces (some days are just better than others) we need to use as many tools in our toolbox as we can, to provide meaning to the work we do every day.

For employers and leaders, understanding how the brain operates – particularly its capacity for neuroplasticity – opens the door to designing more effective workplace cultures that promote well-being, engagement and prosocial behaviours. When we realize that the brain is not fixed but is continually reshaping itself based on the experiences we create, we understand that every policy, programme and interaction has the power to mould not just individual performance but the entire organizational dynamic.

It also reminds us that policies and the leaders who enact them must be agile. Just like the brain, we need to wire and rewire our strategies to meet the moment.

This understanding of neuroscience is a blueprint for unlocking workplace well-being because, like neurons, humans that fire together, wire together. And when we're working together towards a shared goal – a common good – we're inspired, motivated, purpose-driven and happier at work.

HAPPINESS IN ACTION

Battling bias

- Remove identifying information such as names, gender and ethnicity from résumés during the initial screening process.
- Use structured interviews where all candidates are asked the same set of questions, reducing the influence of personal biases during the evaluation.
- Provide training for hiring managers to recognize and address their own biases. Incorporating tools such as Harvard's Implicit Association Test (IAT) can help recruiters become aware of unconscious preferences that may affect their decisions.[35]
- Involve multiple interviewers from diverse backgrounds in the recruitment process. A diverse panel can help check individual biases and ensure a more balanced assessment of candidates.

Attitudes

- Leaders can use storytelling that taps into shared values and emotions to activate neural pathways related to empathy and trust (amygdala and ventral striatum, respectively). This can reduce cultural bias by fostering a sense of connection and understanding across diverse groups.

- Encouraging mindfulness can reduce automatic biased responses by enhancing activity in the pre-frontal cortex, which governs conscious decision-making and emotional regulation, helping to override subconscious bias.

Self-control

- Cognitive reappraisal involves consciously rethinking a situation to see it from a different perspective. For example, I try to practise this when I'm stuck behind someone driving their car at heartbreakingly slow speeds. I've noticed I've become less patient on the road since 2020, and I have to work harder on my emotional regulation these days.

  So, instead of focusing on the delay, I reappraise the situation by thinking, 'This is an opportunity to take a breather.' I'll then hit 'play' on my favourite podcast, which feels like a treat because I mostly listen to my podcasts in the car. By reframing the situation I can reduce feelings of frustration and replace them with a sense of calm or acceptance. It also trains my brain to react differently in the future when I'm in a similar situation.
- This is a cognitive skill that is easily transferable to the workplace. Perhaps a project didn't get completed on time or you didn't get the results you'd expected. Take this as an opportunity to learn and shift your strategy.
- Writing down feelings, especially during emotional distress, can help to process emotions more effectively and understand the triggers behind them. The best part is that it serves as a safe space to express emotions without judgement.
- Simply naming the emotion ('I'm angry', 'I'm anxious') can diminish the intensity of that emotion. It creates a moment of distance between us and the feeling, allowing for better regulation.

Reframing

- Have you and your team spend one week jotting down one thing that happened that day that helped them get their job done. It could be a person that offered support, a new technology that made it easier for them to hit their goals, it just needs to be one thing.
- The following week, write down two or more things that helped make their day easier.

- At the end of the two weeks, get together and share your lists. Use a whiteboard or a flipchart. You can put a tick next to the ones that have an overlap. Often you'll see a person's name with a whole host of tickmarks – definitely a great way to call out those unsung heroes.
- This exercise has many benefits. By writing down two or three things that make their job easier every single day for two weeks, employees will see the ways they are being supported to achieve their objectives. It will also distract their brains from ruminating on all the ways they feel unsupported. Even by the end of the first week, they will start to change the way they think about their self-efficacy now and their approach to these issues in the future.

HAPPY LEARNING!

Isn't learning the best? If you want to go deeper here are my suggestions:

Read

- Emmons, R (2008) *Thanks! How practicing gratitude can make you happier*, Houghton Mifflin
- Hanson, R (2013) *Hardwiring Happiness: The new brain science of contentment, calm and confidence*, Harmony Books
- McGonigal, K (2015) *The Upside of Stress*, Avery

Watch

- Singer, P (2013) The why and how of effective altruism, TED. www.ted.com/talks/peter_singer_the_why_and_how_of_effective_altruism (archived at https://perma.cc/XDM4-TMM4)

Notes

1 Food Forum, Food and Nutrition Board, Institute of Medicine (2015) Interaction between the brain and the digestive system, in *Relationships Among the Brain, the Digestive System, and Eating Behavior: Workshop summary*, National Academies Press. www.ncbi.nlm.nih.gov/books/NBK279994/ (archived at https://perma.cc/VEV4-92PS)

2 Food Forum, Food and Nutrition Board, Institute of Medicine (2015) Interaction between the brain and the digestive system, in *Relationships Among the Brain, the Digestive System, and Eating Behavior: Workshop summary*, National Academies Press. www.ncbi.nlm.nih.gov/books/NBK279994/ (archived at https://perma.cc/VEV4-92PS)

3 University of Texas Permian Basin. What is cognitive bias and how does it affect our lives? University of Texas Permian Basin, nd. online.utpb.edu/about-us/articles/psychology/what-is-cognitive-bias-and-how-does-it-affect-our-lives/#:~:text=The%20human%20brain%20is%20a,juggle%20at%20any%20given%20moment (archived at https://perma.cc/3VML-4JFP)

4 T Bhandari. Mind–body connection is built into brain, study suggests, WashU Medicine, 2023. medicine.washu.edu/news/mind-body-connection-is-built-into-brain-study-suggests/ (archived at https://perma.cc/PN9Q-R2SF)

5 T Okonogi et al. Stress-induced vagal activity influences anxiety-relevant prefrontal and amygdala neuronal oscillations in male mice, *Nature*, 2024. www.nature.com/articles/s41467-023-44205-y (archived at https://perma.cc/93XE-59X6)

6 K Cherry. How does the nervous system work with the endocrine system? VeryWellMind, 2023. www.verywellmind.com/the-nervous-and-endocrine-systems-2794894 (archived at https://perma.cc/G5QF-2S6T)

7 G Raz. Kelly McGonigal: Can we reframe the way we think about stress? NPR, 2019. www.npr.org/transcripts/747384008 (archived at https://perma.cc/U7SX-RPZ5)

8 K McGonigal. Is your mind separate from your body? Psychology Today, 2012. www.psychologytoday.com/ca/blog/the-science-willpower/201208/is-your-mind-separate-your-body (archived at https://perma.cc/4FR4-P7SV)

9 K Cherry. How neuroplasticity works, VeryWellMind, 2024. www.verywellmind.com/what-is-brain-plasticity-2794886 (archived at https://perma.cc/AME3-AFZD)

10 W James (1890). *The Principles of Psychology*, Henry Holt and Company.

11 S Ackerman (1992) The development and shaping of the brain, in *Discovering the Brain*, National Academies Press. www.ncbi.nlm.nih.gov/books/NBK234146/ (archived at https://perma.cc/G8DN-MPK9)

12 J Cacioppo and L Hawkley. Perceived social isolation and cognition, *Trends in Cognitive Science*, 2009, 13, 447–54. 10.1016/j.tics.2009.06.005.

13 R Adolphs. The social brain: Neural basis of social knowledge, *Annual Review of Psychology*, 2009, 60, 693–716. doi: 10.1146/annurev.psych.60.110707.163514. PMID: 18771388; PMCID: PMC2588649.

14 J Hernandez. White-sounding names get called back for jobs more than Black ones, a new study finds, OPB, 2024. www.opb.org/article/2024/04/11/white-sounding-names-get-called-back-for-jobs-more-than-black-ones-a-new-study-finds/ (archived at https://perma.cc/26J2-LSVZ)

15 L Rivera and A Tilcsik. Class advantage, commitment penalty: The gendered effect of social class signals in an elite labor market, *American Sociological Review*, 2016, 81. 10.1177/0003122416668154.

16 M Bogen, All the ways hiring algorithms can introduce bias, *Harvard Business Review*. 2019. hbr.org/2019/05/all-the-ways-hiring-algorithms-can-introduce-bias (archived at https://perma.cc/L5SK-D9DR)

17 S McClure et al. Neural correlates of behavioral preference for culturally familiar drinks, *Neuron*, 2004, 44, 379–87. 10.1016/j.neuron.2004.09.019.

18 H Plassmann, P Kenning, M Deppe and W Kugel. How choice ambiguity modulates activity in brain areas representing brand preference: Evidence from consumer neuroscience, *Journal of Consumer Behaviour*, 2008, 7, 360–67, onlinelibrary.wiley.com/doi/abs/10.1002/cb.257. (archived at https://perma.cc/7K6K-EKS8)

19 N Vences et al. Neuromarketing as an Emotional Connection Tool Between Organizations and Audiences in Social Networks, Frontiers, 2020. www.frontiersin.org/journals/psychology/articles/10.3389/fpsyg.2020.01787/full (archived at https://perma.cc/8FCE-LAP2)

20 J Fitzgerald. Silos that work: How the pandemic changed the way we collaborate, Harvard Business School, 2022. www.library.hbs.edu/working-knowledge/silos-that-work-how-the-pandemic-changed-the-way-we-collaborate (archived at https://perma.cc/6PY5-32G9)

21 S Singh. Twitter (X) user statistics 2024, Demandsage, 2024. www.demandsage.com/twitter-statistics/ (archived at https://perma.cc/W4RE-CDN6)

22 J Novet. How Satya Nadella tripled Microsoft's stock price in just over four years, CNBC, 2018. www.cnbc.com/2018/07/17/how-microsoft-has-evolved-under-satya-nadella.html (archived at https://perma.cc/LJL8-UGJW)

23 W Oremus. The poisonous employee-ranking system that helps explain Microsoft's decline, 2013, Slate. slate.com/technology/2013/08/stack-ranking-steve-ballmer-s-employee-evaluation-system-and-microsoft-s-decline.html (archived at https://perma.cc/T8KW-T7ZA)

24 M Cavanagh et al. The solution-focused approach to coaching, IIABC, 2019. iiabc.org/wp-content/uploads/2019/10/solution-focused-coaching-pages-75-88.pdf (archived at https://perma.cc/K4TT-LY78)

25 D Bridge and K Paller. Neural correlates of reactivation and retrieval-induced distortion, *Journal of Neuroscience*, 2012, 32 (35), 12144–51. doi: 10.1523/JNEUROSCI.1378-12.2012. PMID: 22933797; PMCID: PMC3459586.

26 G Gava et al. Integrating new memories into the hippocampal network activity space, *Nature Neuroscience*, 2021, 24, 326–30. doi.org/10.1038/s41593-021-00804-w (archived at https://perma.cc/R9X9-VK7Y)

27 N Shute. Our brains rewrite our memories, putting present in the past, WVTF, 2014. www.wvtf.org/2014-02-05/our-brains-rewrite-our-memories-putting-present-in-the-past (archived at https://perma.cc/P3GA-JLCZ)

28 E Goldbaum. Research into the nature of memory reveals how cells that store information are stabilized over time, Science Daily, 2024. www.sciencedaily.com/releases/2024/01/240119122657.htm (archived at https://perma.cc/AL6H-LCN8)

29 R Hanson (2013) *Hardwiring Happiness: The new brain science of contentment, calm, and confidence*, Harmony Books.

30 A Javanbakht and L Saab. What happens in the brain when we feel fear, *Smithsonian Magazine*, 2017. www.smithsonianmag.com/science-nature/what-happens-brain-feel-fear-180966992 (archived at https://perma.cc/GZ6X-GGEA)

31 W Schultz. Neuronal reward and decision signals: From theories to data, *Physiological Reviews*, 2015; A Kelley and K Berridge. The neuroscience of natural rewards: Relevance to addictive drugs, *Journal of Neuroscience*, 2002.

32 Wikipedia. Boreout, Wikipedia, nd. en.wikipedia.org/wiki/Boreout (archived at https://perma.cc/DLB6-CXJ5)

33 L Harju, et al. Job boredom and its correlates in 87 Finnish organizations, *Journal of Occupational and Environmental Medicine*, 2014, 56, 911–18.

34 V Jusufi and M Saitovi⊠, How to motivate assembly line workers, tutor: Karl Erik Gustafsson, Jonkoping International Business School, 2007.

35 Harvard. Implicit Association Test, Harvard, nd. implicit.harvard.edu/implicit/takeatest.html (archived at https://perma.cc/9ZZK-K272)

2

The power of habit

We often think happiness is something that happens *to* us – when life finally lines up perfectly, we'll feel it. But I've learned that happiness isn't a destination, it's a practice. And the more I study it, the more I see how we can actively shape it. Our brains are incredibly adaptive, and that's where the magic happens. With the right habits, we can rewire ourselves for happiness.

I want to be clear. We're not talking about grand gestures or overnight changes – just small, consistent shifts that build over time. It's not about choosing happiness but learning how to harness it and extend it in the moment. It's also about unwinding the negative habits that are barriers to well-being. As we build up psychological fitness, we can moderate stress in times of heightened uncertainty and mental strain.

Drawing from the science of neuroplasticity, habits are built by modifying and repeating our behaviours until we can move our conscious actions into our subconscious.

Just as we create daily habits like showering and eating breakfast to maintain a healthy standard of physical hygiene, we also need to practise something I refer to as 'happiness hygiene'. To accomplish a beneficial regime that increases our levels of psychological fitness, we need to start by constructing one habit at a time. This takes time, effort and motivation, but once happiness hygiene is established, the positive impacts are felt almost immediately.

You may be thinking, 'Is this going to take too much time? My life is busy enough already.'

I get it. Well-being shouldn't be workload. To build a happiness habit we need to take it slow. One small baby step at a time. It needs to be short and incremental – a shift that is easy to adapt to in an incredibly busy world.

Developing psychological fitness is a powerful driver of success in the workplace. But when we take it a step further by pairing happiness with habit, we unlock new levels of leadership and elevate our capacity for performance.

The best part about a good habit is that once it is imbedded in the brain it can feel as unnoticeable as buckling our seatbelt or putting on shoes or brushing our teeth. One of the greatest benefits of good habits is that they free up the limited amount of conscious processing available to us in our brain.

Our pre-frontal cortex can decipher what we need to pay attention to through a process of elimination that is beyond what any computer could handle. So, imagine that this amazing processor doesn't have to decide whether to tend to gratitude, or optimism, hope or self-efficacy because the habits have already been formed. The unconscious brain can just keep on trucking while the conscious brain is freed up to make the kinds of decisions leaders are faced with constantly in their roles. We get to hold on to our valuable mental bandwidth for strong, effective leadership – while our subconscious guides us with happiness and altruism at the root of those decisions.

This chapter will be focused on habit-building. Why *we* need to adopt and model these healthy behaviours and why they're valuable to the people we lead. And because bad habits are easy to make and good ones are even easier to break, we'll discuss strategies, tactics and tools to ensure that our happiness habits stick.

Our lazy brains

As we discussed in the last chapter, our brain's plasticity has a substantial part to play in turning our behaviours into habits. Our brain can change, adapt and reorganize itself to optimize our current environment.

Some habits are easier to make than others. According to Daniel Kahneman, the Nobel Prize winning psychologist, the reason for this can be attributed to our brain's 'lazy heuristics'. In psychology, heuristics are simple, efficient rules that we use to form judgements and make decisions. Essentially, our brain wants us to take the easiest path to a solution so we use mental shortcuts to focus on one aspect of a complex problem and ignore others. It also explains why we easily fall back into old patterns.

In the early 1970s, Kahneman, along with his research partner Amos Tversky, challenged the idea that human beings (for the most part) are rational but we estimate our choices by using these shortcuts in the brain. The paper, 'Judgment under uncertainty: Heuristics and biases', discusses how our mental shortcuts can be helpful because they reduce the demand on the brain's resources; 'they are rapid, can be made without full information and can be as accurate as more complicated procedures'.[1] The brain poses many conflicting questions. Is it our lazy brain that helps us to be higher performing, or our powerful processor?

Essentially, it's both. And how we leverage habits, both the positive and the negative ones, will determine how successful we will be as leaders.

If we leverage positive habit building, we can rely on these 'lazy heuristics' to choose the desired path of optimism, hope, gratitude and other traits of the happiest, highest-performing people. However, the same goes for accessing our bad habits. And, as we discussed in previous chapters, our negativity bias strongly influences our brain to behave like we did as early humans – fearful, pessimistic and on high alert. If we just leave our lazy brain to choose then we have to be cognizant of what patterns we want it to select.

We'll spend time over the course of the book to learn how to focus our efforts on building the traits of the highest performing people. But first, let's work on how to form a single habit before we try to make complicated changes. The brain has preferences in its workflow so, whether we want to start flossing our teeth more, eating less at night, walking during meetings or standing up at our desks, we need to learn how to create a simple rubric for developing automaticity with any behaviour.

The myth of the 21-day habit

The reason why it's challenging to build positive habits comes as a result of a variety of challenges. Battling our deeply ingrained negativity bias is already a daily chore, but creating new stimuli, then turning that activity into habitual behaviour, isn't easy. And brains are pretty busy places with no unoccupied space.

In one study, researcher Philippa Lally and her team of scientists studied the process of habit formation in everyday life. Ninety-six volunteers chose a behaviour to carry out daily in the same context for 12 weeks. They completed the Self-Report Habit Index (SRHI) each day and recorded whether they did or did not carry out the behaviour. The time it took participants to reach 95 per cent of their target (behaviour into a habit) ranged from 18 to 254 days. This range is significantly wider and less concrete than the widely held belief that it takes roughly 21 days to build a habit.[2]

This study demonstrated that it takes much longer for a repeated behaviour to reach its maximum level of automaticity (habit). Interventions aiming to create habits require continued support to help us keep that behaviour in habit mode. Philippa Lally commented in her research paper, 'It is interesting to note that even in this study where the participants were motivated to create habits, approximately half did not perform the behaviour consistently enough to achieve habit status.'

What Lally noticed was that simple behaviours were easier to build into habits than complex behaviours. For example, the participants that tried to eat a piece of fruit while at the computer in the evening had a faster path to building the habit, versus the participant who had to do 15 minutes of exercise before dinner every evening. Actually, the exercise habit took one-and-a-half times longer to root than the eating behaviour, supporting the proposal that the complexity of the behaviour impacts the development of a habit.

This study proves that building mental shortcuts won't happen without focus, time and intention. We need to give ourselves and our employees the patience to learn and adopt the positive behaviours that will lead to automaticity.

One of my favourite quotes comes from Biz Stone, the co-founder of Twitter (now X), who said, 'Timing, perseverance, and ten years of trying will eventually make you look like an overnight success.'[3] Stone so aptly describes our societal impatience with success. We intellectually understand that anything worthwhile is worth working for, but we also want everything to happen right now. The fact that the '21 days to a habit' myth could hold on so strongly in popular belief (although it was never proven with any real scientific rigor) emphasizes how we think we can speed up a process just by 'putting our mind to it'.

Quick wins

As leaders, we have to be patient while we build up happiness strategies in our workplace. One of the ways to increase the speed of this effort is to provide quick wins and make the goals small and tangible. Since quick wins are so satisfying to our brains, it makes sense that a series of wins would reap high rewards.

Yet, we must focus on simple and effective strategies versus big, ambitious goals. We should avoid disrupting work too dramatically. We tend to fail at providing quick wins for our employees when the changes we make are too drastic and too fast. And, even with the best intentions, a 'big-goal' strategy tends to backfire. A good way to mitigate this issue is to start by making the effort small, stacked onto a practice that is already habitual at work, and it must be easy to keep up the effort.

Here are a few tangible examples of quick wins:

- An employee makes a presentation at a meeting, and you send over an email recognizing them for their effort. Try setting a calendar appointment reminder to do this for one of your team members every week.
- You have a few extra dollars to spend on company culture, and instead of just spending it on something you think would be fun, ask your team to take a vote and go do that. To make it extra valuable, execute on the decision quickly. If everyone votes to go out for lunch, make it happen right away, even within the week of learning the results. Make this a recurring monthly or quarterly spend.
- Make it a habit to learn something new about one of your employees every month and respond to it immediately. If you're a CEO with thousands of employees it's hard to reach every individual team member. So, empower your managers to be your happiness ambassadors. If your employee loves barbecue food, send them a recommendation for a good restaurant, or a fantastic recipe. If they love rare tea varieties, order some online and have them sent to his or her desk. Does it require effort? Yes. Will it be worth it? Absolutely.

So how can we take these quick wins and turn them into habits? Here's a good place to start.

Stacking habits

Back in 2016 – in the first edition of this book – I wrote about meeting fatigue. I shared how people described it to me as 'time-sucking'. According to David Grady and Jason Fried in a 2014 TED Talk, 'There are more than 3 billion meetings every year, with executives spending 40 to 50 per cent of their total working hours in meetings, with almost 34 per cent of all meetings ending up as wasted time. That loss in productivity is estimated to waste nearly $37 billion every year in the US alone.'[4]

Today, the amount of time wasted in meetings is similar, but the cost is astronomically higher as ineffective meetings now drain $259 billion in the US in lost productivity and $64 billion in the United Kingdom. For the US that's a 600 per cent increase in less than a decade.[5]

Additionally, middle managers report spending around 35 per cent of their work hours in meetings, adding pressure on overall productivity. Plus, workers are spending about half a workday per week just *scheduling* meetings. Since February 2020, people are in three times more Microsoft Teams meetings and calls per week – a 192 per cent increase. And that's just Teams meetings – imagine if we combined this with Zoom, Google Meet, Webex, Amazon's Chime and more, what that would look like!

That time spent in meetings and managing them costs employers an annual average of over $29,000. Coordinating and rescheduling those costs employers an average of over $5,000 annually.[6] The average worker attends about six team and internal meetings a week, about five one-on-one meetings, and about five external meetings. Internal meetings are the most common recurring meeting but also most often rescheduled.

'Time sucking' was the right description, then. I would go so far as to say that it's 'soul sucking' now.

Walk 'n' talks

According to a leading expert, there is a way to make these time-wasting workplace routines a much more enjoyable and productive experience. Visionary and author Nilofer Merchant famously wrote that 'Sitting has become the smoking of our generation'.[7]

In 2015, studies found that we averaged 9.3 hours a day sitting and 7.7 hours sleeping. New research published in the *European Heart Journal* analysed data from more than 15,000 people participating in six studies from five different countries. The study found that people are sleeping the exact same amount as they were a decade ago but the average participant's day now consists of 10.4 hours sitting.[8] Another meta-analysis of over 262,000 adults and 16,000 children found that on average we've increased sitting by 46 minutes since the pandemic started in 2020.[9]

Merchant argued in a TED Talk that 'walking meetings' are the key to more meaningful and productive collaborations. She suggests bringing in alternative technologies to support the effort can increase the adoption rate. When we promote activity with gamification and a sense of competitive fun, it can improve the likelihood of adopting the behaviour and turning it into a habit. And, as a result of pairing an activity like walking, something that used to be considered a 'siloed effort', we combine it with a meeting and *voilà* – exercise becomes meaningful to business outcomes.[10]

I interviewed Nilofer about her work evangelizing walking meetings. She shared that it all started when she met with venture capitalist Heidi Roizen, who'd asked Nilofer to join her on a walking meeting. 'This was her 9 am meeting. While I huffed and puffed more than I would have liked, it made me think… this is a genius idea. So I took it on as a personal habit by scheduling my 4 pm or 5 pm meetings this way. It's a simple shift with a big impact.'

Nilofer also described how her health started to improve from these walking meetings: 'I went from a resting heart rate in the high 60s to a resting heart rate in the high 40s.'

The biggest takeaway from my chat with Nilofer is how she's been changing the mindset of CEOs and how advantageous it's been to these high-ranking executives. Nilofer described one example of a senior leader based in Silicon Valley who now performs all of his one-to-one meetings this way: 'His direct reports say he listens way better and thus the meetings are way more effective… today, our economy is fuelled by ideas, by creativity, by experiences. So what matters is the transfer of insights, and the building up of ideas. You don't do that by being always on with technology, you do that through the best idea technology there is: being present to one another.'

'Forty per cent of our actions are repetitive daily actions,' says Nilofer. 'This is the stuff we don't think about, don't need to put our mental cycles to, but just do. These default actions make up the vast majority of what shapes our days. So, doing walking meetings made something easy by just moving it into the daily act. If you change the small actions, you change your life.'

It was a powerful statement. As a high-performing person Nilofer obviously understands how valuable it is to build positive mental shortcuts. During her 25 years in technology, she personally launched more than 100 products and services – many of which you use daily – netting $18 billion in revenues.

To remain inclusive, I might suggest renaming 'walk 'n' talks' to 'movement meetings' for people with physical disabilities who may face barriers to mobility. Movement can mean simply moving to another space in the building or venturing outside. Taking us away mentally from our current space is the key and stepping away from our desks to get a fresh perspective.

Most vitally, we shift towards a less sedentary lifestyle. One of the ways we can do that is by reducing meeting fatigue. If we want our workforce to be happier, we need to give them their time back. Since we've added so many hours to meeting with each other, we're now forced to work more after hours – in the evenings and on weekends. This is not a recipe for well-being.

Building a boundary habit for healthier work/life harmony

There's a pressure in today's workplace to stay perpetually 'on'. I've seen how quickly this can spiral into what's been called 'toxic productivity'. In an article I wrote for Harvard Business Review, 'Let's End Toxic Productivity', I write how we've developed an overwhelming compulsion to work constantly, even at the expense of mental well-being and relationships.[11] Research backs up what so many of us have experienced first-hand: simply logging more hours doesn't yield more productivity.

Slack's Workforce Index, which analysed more than 10,000 desk workers around the globe, highlights that workers feeling the need to check emails after hours report 20 per cent lower productivity scores. A shocking 67 per cent of directors report having to work overtime due to meeting overload, 76 per cent of respondents feel drained after days packed with meetings, and 80 per cent believe they'd be more productive with less meeting time.[12]

When I think about this, I realize how critical boundaries are for both our health and well-being, *and* our professional performance.

I've found that setting a regular block of protected time for uninterrupted work or simply unwinding can make a world of difference. Instead of saying 'no' to all after-hours tasks, designate specific times where you won't check emails or take calls. When colleagues see that you've protected this time consistently, it sets a precedent for healthier habits.

Laura Giurge, Professor at the London School of Economics, studies the impact of 'time poverty', which means having too many things to do and not enough time to do them. Giurge's research found that employees working on weekends and holidays versus the standard Monday to Friday 9-to-5 hours showed decreased intrinsic motivation. Working after hours caused people to consider better uses of their time – leading to higher attrition.[13]

I think many of us can relate to the cycle of feeling productive only because we're working long hours. But focusing on clear, high-impact outcomes – rather than sheer time spent – can demonstrate the power of prioritization. Tools like task planners or collaborative apps can help with this, especially for high-priority projects. It's about steering away from productivity for productivity's sake and honing in on where our time really matters.

Meeting overwhelm doesn't serve anyone well. A study from 2023 confirms this, with 78 per cent of workers saying they struggle to finish their tasks due to excessive meetings. Another study found... study found that 'employees who feel *obligated* to work after hours suffer from 2.1x worse work-related stress, 1.7x times lower satisfaction with their overall working environment and 2x greater burnout'.[14]

Instead of sitting through back-to-back sessions, alternatives like collaborative documents for updates or smaller breakout meetings can save everyone time and energy. I've also seen how asynchronous tools can be game-changers for productivity. Instead of expecting instant responses on every platform, many teams thrive when given the flexibility to respond on their schedules.

At Microsoft, for instance, shifting to more asynchronous communication gave employees uninterrupted time to concentrate on core tasks, showing that constant availability doesn't always equal productivity.

For leaders, setting boundaries often means rethinking meeting practices. Limiting attendees and focusing on high-impact agendas can prevent team members from feeling overwhelmed. Leaders who excel in fostering healthy boundaries all model the behaviour they encourage, like avoiding emails on weekends or after hours. Salesforce introduced Wellness Wednesdays to encourage time for self-care and focus, and I've seen that a straightforward change like this can resonate deeply with teams.

Flexibility isn't just a perk; it's a key driver of engagement and productivity. Laura Giurge's findings on time poverty reveal that giving employees control over their hours can greatly reduce stress and improve morale. From my experience, flexibility can mean anything from letting employees set their own hours to establishing core meeting times while letting them structure the rest of their day. When autonomy becomes a part of the work culture, productivity benefits naturally follow.

As we navigate a work culture still dominated by constant demands, setting reasonable boundaries is less about restrictions and more about sustainability. Boundaries, after all, aren't barriers; they're enablers of true productivity, allowing both employees and leaders to bring their best, focused selves to work. It's not about doing less – it's about doing what matters most.

When habits go bad

It's important to remember that all habits are not created equal. Negative habits form more easily than positive ones because of how our brains react to stress, fatigue and immediate rewards. Under pressure, our brain releases cortisol, driving us towards actions that provide quick relief. These habits give a temporary dopamine boost, creating a sense of relief that reinforces the behaviour even if it's ultimately unproductive.

By contrast, positive habits such as exercising or meditating don't always offer immediate rewards. Instead, they require a degree of motivation and mental energy that can be harder to rally in moments of stress or exhaustion.

Adding to this is our brain's evolutionary bias for instant gratification, which was useful for survival but doesn't always serve us well in modern life. This tendency means we often favour quick fixes over choices that require patience and delayed gratification.

Environmental cues also reinforce negative habits: the blurring of work and personal life during the pandemic made it easier to fall into patterns like working late, skipping breaks or reaching for comforts. The pandemic also exacerbated negative habits that have today subtly eroded our mental health, happiness and productivity.

Substance use, for example, became a coping mechanism for many dealing with prolonged isolation and uncertainty. Substance use disorders remain elevated in 2024 compared to pre-pandemic levels in 2019, with sustained increases across various types of substance use. What were once used as a temporary relief to isolation and boredom have now turned into disordered behaviours that compound issues like burnout, depression and a general dissatisfaction with work and life.[15] The rise in negative patterning since the pandemic has had a profound impact on workplace well-being, productivity and employee engagement.

Anger and frustration has also seeped into the workplace, a phenomenon some researchers call 'pandemic rage' or 'panger'. This heightened irritability often translates into poorer workplace relationships, decreased cooperation and greater employee disengagement.[16]

Microsoft's Work Trend Index found we're now feeling less connected to our team members, which erodes trust and team cohesion.[17] A sense of isolation coupled with frustration around increased workloads or unclear boundaries has left many employees feeling unsupported and undervalued.

These changes underscore a critical need for healthier work practices and clearer boundaries. Implementing flexible schedules, minimizing unnecessary meetings and actively promoting mental health resources can help.

Building habits for life

Building up the habit of happiness will also come with an invested strategy that looks at culture from a Five to Life approach. Which means, it will take roughly five years of consistent effort to build up the hygiene required for a happier culture. Then it's a lifetime of nurturing it to continue reaping the rewards – even during challenging times.

The '3 Rs' of habit change

From actions like switching on the lights when we enter a room, or looking both ways before we cross the street, or more complex habits like pouring our coffee in the thermal mug before heading to work, or even our ability to tune out of our drive during the morning commute – so many of these daily practices have become ingrained in our subconscious. The saying 'I could do that with my eyes closed' resonates. Why? Because, at any one time we can likely list a dozen or more behaviours we execute without thinking about it.

James Clear describes this pattern as the '3 Rs' of habit change'[18] by which he claims that every habit we make – good or bad – follows the same three-step pattern:

1 Reminder (the trigger that initiates the behaviour).
2 Routine (the behaviour itself; the action you take).
3 Reward (the benefit you gain from doing the behaviour).[19]

In his book *Transform Your Habits*, James provides us with a very clear description of what a habit looks like when broken:

1 Your phone rings (reminder). This is the reminder that initiates the behaviour. The ring acts as a trigger or cue to tell you to answer the phone. It is the prompt that starts the behaviour.
2 You answer your phone (routine). This is the actual behaviour. When your phone rings, you answer the phone.
3 You find out who is calling (reward). This is the reward (or punishment, depending on who is calling). The reward is the benefit gained from doing the behaviour. You wanted to find out why the person on the other end was calling you; discovering that piece of information is the reward for completing the habit.

James claims that if the reward is positive then we'll want to repeat the routine again the next time the reminder happens. Repeat the same action enough times and it becomes a habit. Every habit follows this basic three-step structure.[20]

Test Clear's theory with Nilofer Merchant's advice in mind:

1 **Reminder:** Meetings are constantly on our calendars so it's easy to remind yourself with an environmental cue through the use of calendar prompts. Include a note in the subject line requesting this meeting to be a 'movement meeting'. It makes sense to start with a colleague who you know is on the same page and interested in moving with you.
2 **Routine:** Start by taking one movement meeting every two weeks for three months. Then make it once a week until you can add in another comfortably. It would be ideal to have one movement meeting or more per day, but that might take some time.
3 **Reward:** Pay attention to the cumulative benefits to your mental health and well-being. Have your energy levels increased? Notice the value of the meetings – are they more productive? More creative? Do you find that time spent with colleagues has deepened the friendship? Maybe you want to invite more co-workers to join you? Or keep it as protected time with just you and your co-worker?

To ensure I formed new and improved current leadership habits, I developed my own standard for building habits that stick. The PERSIST model (Figure 2.1) continues to support my happiness routine, and hopefully it can support your efforts as well:

P – Practical: Building a habit isn't about making it into the *Guinness Book of World Records*. Attempting to only eat potatoes for an entire year may or may not be a habit worth building. But trying to increase the automaticity of altruistic behaviour adds so much more value to our lives. Constructive and positive habit building helps us reduce cognitive load – giving us the opportunity to attend to other needs. And by other needs I mean the ones we take for granted, or ignore because we are too emotionally bogged down.

E – Enduring: Keep in mind that building good habits should not reach an end point and looking for that 'out' will actually derail our efforts. Focus instead on thinking about this effort as a permanent change to your ingrained, patterned behaviour. And remember to choose your habits wisely because the change often has a ripple effect.

FIGURE 2.1 The PERSIST model

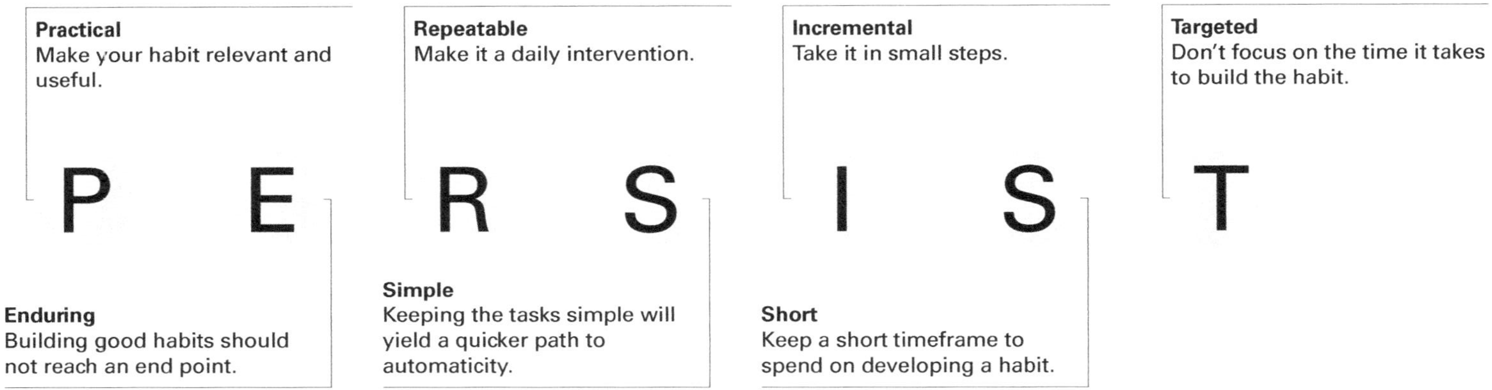

P E R S I S T

Practical
Make your habit relevant and useful.

Enduring
Building good habits should not reach an end point.

Repeatable
Make it a daily intervention.

Simple
Keeping the tasks simple will yield a quicker path to automaticity.

Incremental
Take it in small steps.

Short
Keep a short timeframe to spend on developing a habit.

Targeted
Don't focus on the time it takes to build the habit.

R – Repeatable: Make it a daily intervention. Going back to the benefits of neuroplasticity and those lazy heuristics, we want to get our highest-performing thoughts to travel the easiest neural pathways. If we reinforce a behaviour through repetition, our brain will start to naturally select that behaviour over another. We are not dieting. With effort, we'll aim to change our behaviours permanently.

S – Simple: Keeping the tasks simple will yield a quicker path to automaticity. More complex habits will take longer. It doesn't mean we shouldn't try to attempt more complicated habits; we should just start with quick wins.

I – Incremental: Want to get up earlier? Rather than make a big move and setting your clock for 4 am, start by setting your clock five minutes earlier until the desired wake time has been reached. Incremental changes will develop more sustainable habits than will sweeping changes.

S – Short: Keep the amount of time spent on developing a habit inside a short timeframe. We don't require hours of yoga every day to become more mindful. Start with two minutes of quiet, focused breathing once per day – then twice. It should feel like more of the same activity versus a huge investment of time all at once.

T – Targeted: Make the habit goal specific and measurable. Instead of saying 'I want to get into shape' say 'I want to increase the number of steps I take each day by 200.' Then a week later it's another 200 and so on until you reach the final goal. Don't take on many changes at once – just start with one habit you want to build and you'll be more likely to hit your target goal successfully.

PERSIST has been a terrific way to keep me motivated and on track. And I continue to enjoy all the positive benefits of a more organized personal and professional life. My brain bandwidth is focused on the immediate decisions at hand, and my subconscious brain is reminding me to act with compassion, emotional control, hopefulness, gratitude, resilience and a host of other traits that maintain my happiness on a daily basis.

Now that we have the science to explain how habits are formed in the brain and a few examples of how healthy habits can be formed into everyday behaviours, let's put the learning into practice.

HAPPINESS IN ACTION

1. **Connect with your peers:** Get to know your colleagues better by using your break time to socialize. Once a week when you grab a coffee or a snack, find an opportunity to drop by the desk of someone you're not familiar with and say hello. No need to take more than a couple of minutes, but a quick connection might lead to more opportunities for collaboration.
2. **The habit of thanks:** Before you close your laptop or sign off for the day, send out a thank you email/tweet or text to someone for a job well done. It only has to take two minutes, but it has huge payoffs to your people and also improves your personal well-being.
3. **Walking meetings:** I've explained the science, and how to build the habit. Now it's your turn to take the next meeting standing up or walking around. And no excuses! We often think that we're too far behind on our workload to move from our desk and our work, but the opposite is true. The more we get up and stretch and move, the more productive we are.
4. **The 'habit of you':** Get in the habit of putting yourself first at least once (preferably more – but let's start with once) per day. Take 20 minutes to read something that has no purpose but provides joy. Take five minutes longer to enjoy your coffee without diving into emails. Enjoy a 15-minute nap or quiet time at lunch to reset. Start with small bites of time to give your brain the rest it needs to be productive, innovative and engaged. Emotional control and good leadership come with a well-rested and productive brain. To do that means self-care – something that way too many leaders don't consider as valuable. In my business, that is the most valuable consideration of all.

HAPPY LEARNING!

Read

- Clear, J (nd) How to start new habits that actually stick. jamesclear.com/three-steps-habit-change (archived at https://perma.cc/KRU4-2JHF)
- King, V (2016) *10 Keys to Happier Living*, Headline

Watch

- Merchant, N (2013) Got a meeting? Take a walk. www.ted.com/talks/nilofer_merchant_got_a_meeting_take_a_walk (archived at https://perma.cc/WN3L-G52E)

Notes

1 D Kahneman and A Tversky. Judgment under uncertainty: Heuristics and biases, *Science*, 1974, 185, 4157, 11124–31.

2 P Lally et al. How are habits formed: Modelling habit formation in the real world, *European Journal of Social Psychology*, 2010, 40 (6), 998–1009.

3 Biz Stone. Timing, perseverance, and ten years of trying will eventually make you look like an overnight success, 2017, X. https://x.com/biz/status/936053477414809601?lang=en (archived at https://perma.cc/VGE7-MEXU)

4 D Grady and J Fried. The economic impact of bad meetings, TED, 2014. ideas.ted.com/the-economic-impact-of-bad-meetings (archived at https://perma.cc/RYV2-NK78)

5 D Jolles and G Lorden. When generations meet, LSE, nd. www.lse.ac.uk/tii/assets/documents/When-Generations-Meet.pdf (archived at https://perma.cc/TD7C-AJCM)

6 H Mensik. The true cost of meetings, by the numbers, worklife, 2024. www.worklife.news/culture/the-true-cost-of-meetings-by-the-numbers/ (archived at https://perma.cc/PEY3-9WFB)

7 N Merchant. Sitting is the smoking of our generation, *Harvard Business Review*, 2013. hbr.org/2013/01/sitting-is-the-smoking-of-our-generation (archived at https://perma.cc/BBD6-URMM)

8 J Corliss. How much do you sit, stand, and move each day? Harvard Health Publishing, 2024. www.health.harvard.edu/heart-health/how-much-do-you-sit-stand-and-move-each-day (archived at https://perma.cc/2PF2-K2QK); J M Blodgett et al. Device-measured physical activity and cardiometabolic health, *European Heart Journal*, 2024. pubmed.ncbi.nlm.nih.gov/37950859 (archived at https://perma.cc/H59U-U2MV)

9 A Runacre et al. Impact of the Covid-19 pandemic on sedentary time and behaviour in children and adults: A systematic review and meta-analysis, *International Journal of Environmental Research and Public Health*, 2021, 18 (21), 11286. www.mdpi.com/1660-4601/18/21/11286 (archived at https://perma.cc/L86A-GNYV)

10 N Merchant. Got a meeting? Take a walk, Ted, 2013. www.ted.com/talks/nilofer_merchant_got_a_meeting_take_a_walk?subtitle=en (archived at https://perma.cc/WS3N-T92T)

11 Let's End Toxic Productivity, *Harvard Business Review*, November 2024, https://hbr.org/2024/11/lets-end-toxic-productivity (archived at https://perma.cc/PH95-DFC8)

12 Slack. The surprising connection between after-hours work and decreased productivity, Slack, 2023. slack.com/blog/news/the-surprising-connection-between-after-hours-work-and-decreased-productivity (archived at https://perma.cc/38WL-GM4M)

13 L Giurge. Beyond material poverty: Why time poverty matters for individuals, organisations, and nations, University of Oxford, nd. wellbeing.hmc.ox.ac.uk/publications/beyond-material-poverty-why-time-poverty-matters-for-individuals-organisations-and-nations (archived at https://perma.cc/DW5F-7KD7)

14 Slack. The surprising connection between after-hours work and decreased productivity, Slack, 2023. slack.com/blog/news/the-surprising-connection-between-after-hours-work-and-decreased-productivity (archived at https://perma.cc/38WL-GM4M)

15 A Roberts et al. Alcohol and other substance use during the Covid-19 pandemic: A systematic review, *Drug Alcohol Depend*, 2021, 229(Pt A):109150. doi: 10.1016/j.drugalcdep.2021.109150. PMID: 34749198; PMCID: PMC8559994.

16 A Dyslin. Does the pandemic have you 'pangry'? Newsnetwork, 2022. newsnetwork.mayoclinic.org/discussion/does-the-pandemic-have-you-pangry (archived at https://perma.cc/LD3N-RDSV)

17 Microsoft. Work Trend Index: Hybrid work as a new cultural norm, Microsoft, 2022. news.microsoft.com/en-cee/2022/04/04/work-trend-index-hybrid-work-as-a-new-cultural-norm (archived at https://perma.cc/NN4X-VGNR)

18 J Clear. The 3 Rs of habit change: How to start new habits that actually stick, James Clear, nd. www.jamesclear.com/three-steps-habit-change (archived at https://perma.cc/V324-V5SF) (archived at https://perma.cc/KRU4-2JHF)

19 J Clear. The 3 Rs of habit change: How to start new habits that actually stick, James Clear, nd. www.jamesclear.com/three-steps-habit-change (archived at https://perma.cc/V324-V5SF)

20 J Clear (2014) *Transform Your Habits*, James Clear.

3

Emotional intelligence and leadership

If previous chapters haven't clearly emphasized the point that human beings relate to each other and the external world through emotional connections, I'll make sure to repeat that now. Positive relationships make us happy. This is not limited to relationships within our families and our core friendship groups. We actually develop relationships with everything we interact with. From the food we eat, to the purchases we make and how we work.

We are all innately emotional human beings. Trying to work against those emotions is counterproductive, and yet creating those relationships with people inside of our companies can prove to be challenging. It is even more challenging when we follow the old patterns of establishing workplace relationships.

When we're separated by hierarchical systems, schematically laid out with organizational charts, gaps can be felt between and amongst the levels inside an organization. Leaders can easily wind up separated from their teams and even their peers. This inevitably creates a disconnect so decisions are made without all the data. If you're not spending time in your people's world, you get out of touch.

We've seen this play out across the workforce in recent years, with hashtags like #quitok and 'rage quitting' synonymous with the Gen Z rebellion. But it's not just this generation who is revolting. When CEOs of major global firms started to call workers back into the office five days a week, there were public outcries with employees asking, 'Where's the data?'

Most leaders are exhausted by this growing unrest and divisiveness but it's challenging to get on the same page with your team if your executive leadership isn't aligned with them. I've spoken to many senior leaders who describe a longing for more interactions with their staff and nostalgia for the days when the relationship between leaders and teams was less strained.

To find a way back to each other we need to remember that whether we are a 'them' or an 'us', in our most simplified form we're all still human beings. In an era of rapidly rising AI and technology automation we must expand our emotional intelligence (EI) now more than ever. EI in AI is the difference between future competitiveness and future obsolescence.

This chapter will expand on how emotional intelligence builds better leaders, and why employees relate and perform better inside organizations with high emotional intelligence. We will look at the organizations that have long been investing in the study and research of emotional intelligence and why it's their best-kept secret. We'll also define the term more fully. We will learn how to engage in the behaviours that lead to the highest levels of emotional intelligence and then define ways to integrate those understandings in our day-to-day life at work and at home.

According to Mayer et al, psychologists and the pioneers of the emotional intelligence movement, 'Emotional intelligence involves the ability to perceive accurately, appraise, and express emotion... to generate feelings when they facilitate thought... to understand emotion and emotional knowledge; and... regulate emotions to promote emotional and intellectual growth'.[1]

Globally recognized psychologist Daniel Goleman, author of the *New York Times* bestsellers *Emotional Intelligence* and *Social Intelligence: The new science of human relationships*, plays an influential role in the popularization of emotional intelligence in leadership and business environments. For many years, Goleman, a science journalist at the *New York Times*, reported on the brain and behavioural sciences. He was responsible for aligning the Dalai Lama with scientific researchers and academics to underline how leadership, creativity, performance and emotional intelligence are connected.

Goleman was also instrumental in discovering how social emotional learning (SEL) could help improve academic achievement. When students were measured across grade averages and testing scores, self-awareness, confidence, managing disturbing emotions and impulses, plus increases in empathy, it was determined that all academic metrics improved.[2]

In a meta-analysis of 668 evaluation studies conducted by Roger Weissberg at the University of Illinois at Chicago, the data showed that programming in SEL would generate an increase in achievement scores by up to 50 per cent, and up to 38 per cent improved their grade-point averages. And programmes also made students and schools safer. According to the study, 'incidents of misbehaviour dropped by an average of 28 percent; suspensions by 44 percent; and other disciplinary actions by 27 percent. At the same time, attendance rates rose, while 63 percent of students demonstrated significantly more positive behavior'.[3]

In the realm of psychology, when outcomes like this arise out of research with youth, we can often expect it to be extrapolated further into the benefits for adults. Goleman's research sketched out the framework for how social emotional learning ties to brain science. He uncovered that the increased learning can be attributed to improvements in attention and working memory, key functions of the pre-frontal cortex. It would also suggest that neuroplasticity and building the habits of happiness would play a key role in the benefits of social emotional learning.

According to Daniel Goleman, leadership and employee development are similar to how we educate young people in SEL at school, but focused on adults at work. So why wouldn't similar results apply?

Companies like Johnson & Johnson, part of Daniel Goleman's research, found that employees with high leadership potential were far stronger in emotional intelligence. From youth to adults, in most cases data suggests that increased social emotional intelligence will improve performance. The trick is to focus the learning development further upstream.

The distinction between the terms 'upstream' and 'downstream' in the context of psychological interventions is essential knowledge. I mention it consistently in my writing, during my talks and when I support companies with their culture strategies. I believe that the reason so many well-being and culture strategies fail is a result of overly focusing on downstream tactics instead of building out sustainable upstream strategies. In *The Burnout Epidemic*, I suggest that self-care alone won't solve for the institutional stressors – like overwork and lack of agency and recognition – that cause chronic stress. In *Why Are We Here?* I suggest the workforce has fundamentally changed after facing their mortality during the Covid-19 pandemic, and ignoring this paradigm shift will create an economic catastrophe.

Here, I want to get us in the habit of asking ourselves, 'Is this an upstream solution or a downstream tactic?' whenever we're making strategic pivots, it will be the foundational differentiation point in the way we build out our culture. The more we consider happiness and emotional intelligence as the roots of those strategies, the more success we will enjoy.

These broadly used terms can be applied to a variety of fields, but in this circumstance and throughout the book we'll refer to it as a place in time when interventions occur.

To further illustrate, the upstream/downstream distinction is well explained by John McKinlay, a medical sociologist. Over 50 years ago he presented 'A case for refocusing upstream: The political economy of sickness', a paper that changed the way we think about the timing of interventions today. In it, he shares a parable of a physician who continues to rescue people from drowning in a fast-moving current. Each time the physician pulls someone out of the river and saves them, another person floats by in need of his help. As he's busy saving their lives, he continues to miss the opportunity to run upstream and stop them from falling in.[4]

McKinlay perfectly describes how we frequently focus our efforts on the downstream interventions. And although many of those interventions are still effective at reacting to a need, if we only invest in reactionary measures we can't invest our time further upstream to get to the root of the need.

This occurs constantly in the workplace.

Let's do a test here. How many of you reading this book participate in a looking-back, one-point-in-time survey – for example, the annual engagement survey?

Would you say that's an upstream or a downstream metric? If you said downstream, you would be correct.

When we measure an outcome rather than an input, we rarely get the whole picture on engagement inside our organizations. How do we know if someone didn't have a frustrating conversation with their co-worker minutes before answering the survey? Or they have answered this same survey each year and nothing has changed? They could be feeding the survey false information. Also, most people don't answer truthfully for fear of being 'found out' if they answer it honestly.

If you are more focused on building up the skills of emotionally intelligent teams and measure more frequently, you'll see a much more honest and accurate picture of organizational health. But don't take it from me. Here are some examples of those early adopters of EI-driven worker strategies and how it's playing out.

The early adopters

If I asked which organization was the first to investigate the benefit of emotionally intelligent teams to their business outcomes, would you know the answer? And could you guess when those initiatives began?

Surprisingly (or perhaps not surprisingly to some), the answer is the US Navy. Although it would take until the 80s before emotional intelligence had a name, the Navy's evaluation and practice of emotional intelligence dates all the way back to World War II. And, since these early discoveries, they've been active as leaders in research, the first to create internal budgets, recruit based on specific psychometric profiling, train talent, develop academic curricula and use data to measure success.

The US Navy and its effort to unlock happiness and high performance has been at the forefront of dozens of research investigations. One specific study, 'The relationship between emotional intelligence and leader performance' by Major Michael Trabun of the United States Marine Corps, may explain why we keep focusing on the downstream effects and remain averse to connecting emotionally with our people.[5]

Major Trabun believes that we have deeply ingrained biases about emotional leadership and it is even more entrenched in military roles than, arguably, any other industry. For some time now, the language of leadership and emotions have not been synonymous and the assumed bias of emotional leadership tends to be a negative one.

From CEOs to army officers, unfortunately there has been a prevailing philosophy that to be an effective leader one must reduce the role that emotions play in problem solving or decision-making. In military culture, soldiers and military personnel are asked to make quick decisions in chaotic environments, and therefore, as Major Trabun explains, the old way of thinking was that, 'allowing for emotion as part of a decision-making process, can bring about potentially negative consequences. As a result, the military leader is one who most likely has learned to subdue or separate the influence that emotions play in any situation'.

In actuality, the US military soon determined the opposite to be true of the above theory.

With scientific research dating back to the Second World War, we are more equipped now to explain how emotions play a positive role in leadership events. As this research continues to be publicly consumed, we see the existing biases shift. Although we still see a prevalence of stoicism in leadership personas, it's slowly starting to change. No longer does it feel contradictory to believe that a leader or manager can effectively use emotions for more consistent and positive outcome with peers, subordinates, stakeholders and higher-ups.

At first, the US Navy's main objective wasn't to increase their personnel's happiness; rather, they were looking to improve their performance. When personnel returned from war, it was apparent that they were suffering from what we now know as post-traumatic stress disorder (PTSD), eventually defined in the DSMIII in 1980. However, this 'pain of the mind' was a real threat to our health and our performance long before we understood it to be PTSD.

During the two world wars of the twentieth century, the military was attempting to resolve what was referred to as 'shell shock'. By December 1914 up to 10 per cent of officers were suffering from shell shock, and 40 per cent of casualties from the Battle of the Somme were shell shocked.[6] The term 'shell shock', however, created some controversy because it seemed to suggest that the brain was traumatized physically while some were also traumatized psychologically. It would later be only discovered that, of 2,000 cases of shell shock, there were many examples that did not directly involve explosions and yet the emotional and physical pain were undeniably visible.[7]

As you can see, the US Navy's desire to better understand how personnel returned from war would lead to a deeper investigation and investment in research to understand the impact of emotional intelligence of a military employee. And, subsequently, that knowledge would transfer to the general public, prompting more discussions about employee engagement and overall workplace happiness.

New research by Martin Seligman shows how the US military is continuing to evolve this conversation related to the benefit of psychologically fit soldiers. At the BetterUp Conference in 2023, conference in 2023 he shared how this new research came to be:

> In 2008, General George Casey, the chief of staff of the United States Army, called me to a meeting of the General Staff in the Pentagon. And he said to me, 'Dr Seligman, post-traumatic stress disorder, suicide, drug abuse, divorce, panic, what does positive psychology tell us about that?'
>
> And I said, 'Well, sir, people's reaction to bad events like combat or other difficult life events is bell-shaped. And you've just described the left-hand side of the bell. You've described the people who collapse under fire. It's important to remember that in the middle is what we call ordinary human resilience. That people may show temporary PTSD symptoms, but, three months later, they're gone and people are functioning well.'

Seligman went on to describe how the right-hand side is post-traumatic growth. People may go through severe PTSD for several months, but a year later, by physical and psychological measures, they're stronger than they were to begin with. He says this is equally common as PTSD.

> I said, 'What resilience and positive psychology are about is moving that whole distribution to the right, moving it in the direction of post-traumatic growth.' Whereupon, General Casey said, 'My legacy of the United States Army is going to be to create an army that is just as psychologically fit as physically fit.'

Seligman and General Casey developed what became known as Comprehensive Soldier Fitness. The research started with a co-created hundred item questionnaire about psychological variables that all soldiers take on the first day. They analysed 78,000 soldiers deployed to Iraq and Afghanistan of which 5 per cent were diagnosed with PTSD. But they also measured the entire military organization, which ended up being 990,000 people from IT to PR, for over five years.

There were two measures that were relevant. The first is high versus low combat stress. The higher the combat stress, the more likely PTSD. But almost as important was catastrophic thinking. Six of the items on the questionnaire are the extremeness of the battle. For example, 'When bad things occur to me, everything unravels.' First, people in the bottom quartile of that question are 370 per cent more likely to develop PTSD when they face severe combat. 'This basically tells you who to avoid putting into severe situations,' says Seligman. Second, the low 'catastrophizers', the people who were in the top quartile of this question, do very well under high-pressure circumstances.

Three things predicted high levels of success and resilience under duress. 'First is high optimism, second is high positive emotion, and third is low negative affect, low complaining,' Seligman says.

What is critical for us to know here is that we can develop these skills in our workforce. Part of this is a reminder of what we just went through and how much of these skills we've already built up. Think about it: cognitive optimism is believing that everything will turn out OK even it didn't go as planned. How many of us had to pivot and continue to pivot today in response to another disruption that is out of our control. We may not realize it but responding in a productive way and taking the change as it comes is optimism skill-building.

We need to remind ourselves that we have more power than we think we do. When we recognize how far we've come, it helps us to build up more positive emotion that then translates into more positive narratives circulating our workplace environments.

This means taking some time to reflect and share stories with each other. But sharing the right ones makes it a reframing versus a rumination exercise.

Putting the pandemic in the rear-view can help us avoid the negative emotions – but if we don't see that there was also some value we just waste a crisis. Take some time with your team to consider what you've learned together and how that has shaped you for the better.

And finally, if you're questioning whether you'll look weak if you make emotional intelligence a strategic priority, check first with General Casey. He'll have the answer.

Looking upstream

Examining the experience of the US Navy and the US military, we'll notice that most organizations in the past were looking to improve business outcomes first, and employee wellness last. Sadly, today we are still watching metrics like engagement and productivity, or absenteeism and presenteeism, as the measure for well-being. I also see surveys that are measuring burnout and stress, but only scratching the surface of what that really means inside their organizations.

Unfortunately, they often wind up being false measures. Most high-performing organizations will see data that shows engagement and burnout at the exact same levels.

Again, taking the case study of the US military; they wanted to ensure their personnel were better equipped to re-enter the battlefield in a healthier, more resilient version of themselves. Training in emotional intelligence wasn't even on their radar, but as they began investing in the well-being of their employees, the payoff was fewer soldiers with post-traumatic stress. It wasn't until they saw the payback to their investment that it became a future strategy. Their response to solving the problem highlights how most organizations treat the symptoms of disengagement instead of proactively reducing the downstream negative effects through prophylactic interventions.

Addressing problems downstream is a highly inefficient route to successful business outcomes. The same antiquated attitude prevails amongst too many organizational leaders. A double bottom line, whereby an organization seeks to extend the bottom line that measures fiscal performance by adding a second bottom line that measures positive social impact, is still perceived as a 'nice to have' versus a 'must have'.

But there are some leaders who just get it. Here is one such example.

Doubling down on a double bottom line

Alexandre L'Heureux, which fittingly translates to Alexandre the Happy, is a leader who lives up to his name. He has exemplified how a leader can blend high performance with a strong commitment to employee well-being. Since becoming CEO of WSP Global Inc in 2016, he has transformed a small Montreal-based engineering firm into a $32 billion industry leader while ensuring that workplace culture remains just as important as financial success.

Under his leadership, WSP's stock surged 500 per, and revenues grew by 125 per cent, reaching $14.4 billion. But what makes WSP truly remarkable is not just its financial performance – it's how L'Heureux has cultivated a thriving, engaged workforce of 73,000 employees, who are collectively working on 200,000 projects across every continent, including Antarctica.

L'Heureux understands that a company's culture is just as vital as its strategy. His approach to leadership is rooted in creating a work environment where employees feel connected, motivated, and supported. He fosters team cohesion through direct engagement with employees, encouraging leaders to spend time in the field, listen to teams, and remove barriers to success. His philosophy is simple: performance thrives in a culture of trust, camaraderie, and shared purpose.

One of his personal passions is chess, which strongly reflects his leadership style. He plays thousands of games a year and even works with a young coach to refine his strategic thinking. This dedication to lifelong learning, adaptability, and anticipation of future moves mirrors how he leads WSP, ensuring that employees embrace growth, innovation, and resilience.

Beyond strategy, L'Heureux believes in maintaining an environment where work is not just about output, but also about engagement and enjoyment. WSP encourages team-building initiatives, mentorship programs, and leadership development to create a workplace where employees feel valued and inspired. This commitment to well-being is not just anecdotal – companies that prioritize employee happiness see measurable gains, with research from the University of Warwick finding that happy employees are 12 per cent more productive, while unhappy ones see a 10 per cent drop in performance.[8]

L'Heureux's success at WSP proves that profitability and people-centric leadership are not mutually exclusive. His ability to balance financial growth with a culture of engagement, well-being proves that a double bottom line is worth the effort.

The competitive advantage

I had the privilege of interviewing Shawn Achor, a global leader in the positive psychology discussion. Shawn is the author of *The Happiness Advantage* and *Before Happiness*, a former Harvard Professor and a teacher of several classes related to happiness in collaboration with Oprah. Shawn also happens to consult 41 of the Fortune 100 companies about leading with happiness. I asked Shawn why it is so important for us to lead with happiness and emotional intelligence. He responded by sharing an example of how that conversation is shifting amongst the companies he consults.

He said, 'Leaders have a myopic view of their role, and they are not taking into account the key motivators to performance. In today's workforce, there are dramatic generational gaps and success looks very different amongst those groups. We see new talent coming into the workforce and they are expecting a shift in cultural consciousness. They want to know, 'Where can I apply my talent?' 'Which company can develop me personally?' If we don't figure out how to make this happen inside our organizations, and if we lack the emotional intelligence to figure out how to unlock their potential, we'll stop being competitive.

'I'm most intrigued with how we can sustain the happiness movement and change the dialogue around well-being in companies. For so long we have talked about finding that elusive work/life balance, but over the past eight years I've seen the conversation shift towards integrating the whole person and making decisions that are sustainable not only for the company, but for the individual. Those companies that embrace this perspective are at the forefront of talent retention and engagement and, I believe, will lead a revolution in the way that we think about human resources.'

Why is it so hard to invest in happiness?

Far too many people think a happiness strategy is just a 'feel good' initiative rather than a profitable plan. The intangibility of it constrains our ability to trust that concepts like building emotionally intelligent leaders or increasing hope and optimism amongst our teams will prove out through financial measurement. We don't believe that happiness translates into hitting financial goals or achieving key performance metrics in any real way.

Why?

Because most leaders don't measure their happiness strategies and therefore don't have the data to prove it.

However, psychologist David McClelland learned through his research that when senior managers in Fortune 500 companies had high emotional intelligence, their divisions outperformed yearly earnings goals by 20 per cent.[9]

A study of US Air Force recruiters showed that those recruiters with high emotional intelligence scores exceeded 100 per cent of their annual recruitment quotas. And, by using emotional intelligence in their hiring practices, the Air Force would see their financial losses cut by 92 per cent, or almost $2.8 million.[10]

Shawn Achor has been studying the financial outcomes of happiness strategies for years and does an excellent job of explaining the value of tying happiness and emotional intelligence to business outcomes:

> In high school science classes, we still teach that you are just your genes and your environment. Our society lives imprisoned by the belief that change is not possible and we live under the tyranny of genes and environment. But over a decade of research in positive psychology is crystal clear: there is a third path. By consciously changing our mindset and cultivating simple two-minute habits, we can trump the effect of our genes and environment over happiness. Scientifically, happiness is a choice, and when we make that choice, it is contagious within our organizations and families. Moreover, the greatest competitive advantage in the modern economy is a positive and engaged brain. When the brain is positive, productivity rises by 31 per cent, revenues can triple, likelihood of promotion rises 40 per cent and sales rise by 37 per cent.

One of the contributors to our happiness is psychological safety – the concept that individuals feel safe to take interpersonal risks – such as asking questions, sharing ideas, or admitting mistakes, without fear of negative consequences to their self-image, status or career. This environment of trust and openness is crucial for fostering innovation, engagement and collaboration in workplaces, as it allows employees to fully participate and contribute without fear of judgement. The concept of psychological safety was extensively studied by Amy Edmondson, a professor at Harvard Business School. In her pioneering work, Edmondson demonstrated that psychological safety is a critical factor in team performance. Through her research, Edmondson found that teams with high psychological safety are more effective because members are comfortable admitting errors and seeking feedback, which are key behaviours for continuous improvement and problem-solving.[11]

Edmondson's research, notably her 1999 paper 'Psychological safety and learning behavior in work teams', revealed that when employees feel psychologically safe, they are more likely to engage in learning behaviours like seeking feedback, sharing information, and experimenting with new ideas. She has since expanded her research, showing how psychological safety is essential not just for individual growth but for creating resilient, adaptable organizations.[12]

The freedom of authenticity

Psychological safety also encourages people to act more authentically which fosters happier workplaces. Partnering on a survey with Jim Moss, co-founder and Chief Strategy Officer at The Work Better Institute, Dr Vanessa Buote, Post-Doctoral Fellow at Wilfrid Laurier University and Dr Anne Wilson, Professor of Psychology at Wilfrid Laurier University, we asked how authentic respondents feel in their workplace and how that plays out in a variety of ways with regards to their performance.

When we looked at the correlations between authenticity and improved workplace experiences, this is what we learned. Authentic employees, those who felt they were sharing their true self at work, had higher levels of well-being and thriving. The research found that employees:

- were less stressed at work
- were more satisfied with their jobs
- were happier while at work
- were more grateful for their work
- felt a stronger sense of community at work
- were more engaged
- were more inspired

When we asked, 'Why is it important to be your true self at work?' here are some of the answers we received:

- no hiding
- less censoring
- less energy spent focusing on self-presentation and more energy spent on being productive
- better relationships in the workplace

So, what kind of workplace helps employees to be authentic?

According to Dr Vanessa Buote, the expression of one's authentic self is largely related to whether people feel comfortable, or whether it's acceptable, to express their true self at work. On average, people reported that it took about two to three months to show their true self at work. By the three-month mark, 60 per cent were authentic, and by nine months 81 per cent were showing their true selves. Only 9 per cent reported that it took more than one year at their position to be authentic.

Dr Buote's report stated:

> The vast majority of people (80 percent) who felt they were being authentic at work believed that it improves the workplace. When asked why they felt it made the workplace better, comments tended to center around a few key themes; they had to exert less energy and time censoring or hiding themselves (31 percent) and that authenticity improved productivity and increased success (33 percent). These themes were frequently tied together, such that because employees were spending less time/energy self-monitoring, more time and energy was spent focusing on the task at hand.

Some of the comments included:

> 'Because it takes a lot of time and effort to act like someone that you aren't. Being my true self at work makes me happy. I do better work when I am happy.'
>
> 'By being my true self, I can 100 percent delve into my work without constantly censoring myself, which can be so draining.'
>
> 'It takes effort to portray a "work persona". This is largely wasted effort. The common requirement to portray a different "professional persona" is anachronistic and counter-productive.'
>
> 'You are able to develop your true skills and strengths, and work on your areas of opportunity – you can only improve on your weaknesses by admitting they are there.'
>
> 'Every person has the need to feel connected to the work they produce. That feeling of connection is attained when employees are encouraged to be themselves and to use their unique talents to create something awesome.'
>
> 'Because being genuine helps me connect with my customers, suppliers and partners. Even in the internet age, people still buy from people.'

Dr Vanessa Buote wrapped up her report with the following commentary:

> Displaying our true self can bring down barriers and free up our mental energy to boost productivity. I would caution that it's also important to find a balance

> between showing our true self and respecting others and their boundaries. We don't need to hide emotions or weaknesses but we do need to ensure that we're not negatively affecting anyone.

My advice to the CEOs I work with is, get closer to who you want to be – vulnerability is a core strength not a weakness. And being authentic encourages others to be their true selves, which is better for business.

Dr Buote agrees. 'We're all unique. Don't be afraid to show it.'

In Chapter 4 we'll discuss how to translate emotional intelligence into business intelligence through the lens of compassionate capitalists, with interviews from Raj Sisodia, CEO of Compassionate Capitalism, and others who are forming a new wave of business leaders that are investing in a double bottom line approach to running their companies.

Before we flip the page and start discussing this very important follow-up topic, let's take a few minutes to keep up the habit of high performance.

HAPPINESS IN ACTION

If I could I would

- Imagine you had a budget of $100. What would you do to make one small change inside your organization? Write down what you would do and why it would make a difference.
- Now, imagine you had $10,000 and $100,000 and repeat the activity.
- What is it that is holding you back from executing on any one of these plans?

Focus on five

- List five specific and actionable examples of how you could be a more emotionally intelligent leader.
- Implement those actions and keep a diary of how it was actualized and subsequently perceived by your employees.

HAPPY LEARNING!

Read

- Achor, S (2011) *The Happiness Advantage: The seven principles of positive psychology that fuel success and performance at work*, Virgin
- Achor, S (2013) *Before Happiness: The five hidden keys to achieving success, spreading happiness, and sustaining positive change*, Crown Business
- Bradberry, T and Greaves, J (2009) *Emotional Intelligence 2.0*, TalentSmart
- Edmondson, A (2018) *The Fearless Organization: Creating psychological safety in the workplace for learning, innovation, and growth*, Wiley
- Kahneman, D (2011) *Thinking, Fast and Slow*, Farrar, Straus and Giroux

Notes

1 J Mayer et al. Human abilities: Emotional intelligence, *Annual Review of Psychology*, 2008, 59, 507–36. 10.1146/annurev.psych.59.103006.093646.

2 D Goleman. The secret to success, *Education Digest: Essential readings condensed for quick review*, 2008.

3 J Durlak et al. The impact of enhancing students' social and emotional learning: A meta-analysis of school-based universal interventions, *Child Development*, 2011, 82 (1), 405–32. doi: 10.1111/j.1467-8624.2010.01564.x. PMID: 21291449.

4 J McKinlay (1975) A case for refocusing upstream: The political economy of sickness, in J Enelow and J Henderson (eds), *Applying Behavioral Science to Cardiovascular Risk*, American Heart Association, 9–25.

5 M A Trabun. The relationship between emotional intelligence and leader performance, US Naval Postgraduate School, 2002. archive.org/details/therelationshipb109456007 (archived at https://perma.cc/566V-9MWN)

6 C Anders. From 'irritable heart' to 'shellshock': How post-traumatic stress became a disease, Gizmodo, 2012. gizmodo.com/from-irritable-heart-to-shellshock-how-post-trauma-5898560 (archived at https://perma.cc/MB42-4TFU)

7 C Myers. Shell shock in France 1914–18 based on a war diary, *JAMA*, 1940, 115 (18),1573. doi:10.1001/jama.1940.02810440065030

8 Andrew J Oswald, Eugenio Proto and Daniel Sgroi. Happiness and productivity. *Journal of Labor Economics*, 33 (4) 2015, pp. 789–822.

9 D McClelland and R Koestner (1992) The achievement motive, in *Motivation and Personality*, ed C P Smith et al, Cambridge University Press.

10 C Cherniss and D Goleman (2001) *The Emotionally Intelligent Workplace: How to select for, measure, and improve emotional intelligence in individuals, groups, and organizations*, Wiley.

11 A Edmondson (2018) *The Fearless Organization: Creating psychological safety in the workplace for learning, innovation, and growth*, Wiley.

12 A Edmondson. Psychological safety and learning behavior in work teams, *Adminstrative Science Quarterly*, 1999. journals.sagepub.com/doi/abs/10.2307/2666999 (archived at https://perma.cc/5Y4X-GY5J)

4

Conscious capitalism

Conscious capitalism requires us to shift the business focus from 'profit at any cost' to 'profit with a purpose'. The idea is simple but powerful: businesses don't just exist to make money; they exist to serve, to uplift and to create value for everyone involved – employees, customers, communities and even the planet.

In conscious capitalism, a business is built on four pillars: higher purpose, stakeholder orientation, conscious leadership and conscious culture. Companies that embrace this model seek both financial success and a positive social or environmental impact. This isn't about adding a few feel-good policies; it's about embedding a sense of purpose and responsibility into every layer of the organization.

Take companies like Ben & Jerry's. They integrate social justice and environmental responsibility into their business model, supporting fair trade and progressive causes. I may even suggest they have a triple bottom line because their ice cream delivers pure happiness. Conscious capitalism doesn't mean sacrificing profits; in fact, research consistently shows that companies with strong, purpose-driven cultures tend to outperform financially over time. It's an approach that rewards everyone involved and drives meaningful, sustainable growth.

So, as we rethink the role of business in society, conscious capitalism offers a roadmap – a way for companies to thrive and make a difference. It's about aligning profit with purpose and proving that doing well and doing good is worth doing.

What is conscious capitalism?

You may be familiar with the term corporate social responsibility (CSR), popularized in the 1960s, which is a set of initiatives a company can implement alongside their existing business practices. CSR engages in 'actions that appear to further some social good, beyond the interests of the firm and that which is required by law'.[1] CSR strategies encourage the company to make a positive impact on the environment and stakeholders including consumers, employees, investors, communities and others.

Conscious capitalism is simply an advancement of the concept of CSR but it evolved to a more holistic way of thinking about the term.

Its evolution came as a result of tying metrics and expectations to decipher whether the philosophy was tied to all areas of your business. As CSR would be an aspect of your organization, possibly siloed in its efforts and thought of as a cost centre, conscious capitalism is reflected in who you are and how you behave across your entire organization.

This ideology shifts all aspects of an organization to refocus its efforts on people first and economics after. That doesn't mean that output isn't measured, it just mandates a holistic way of defining success, and those metrics aren't all financial.

Muhammad Yunus, who in 2006 won the Nobel Peace Prize for his social and economic development work in Bangladesh, first used the term conscious capitalism.[2] Yunus, a Professor of Economics, founded the Grameen Bank in 1976, which focused on giving poor Bangladeshi people, especially women, access to micro credit to start micro businesses. Yunus hypothesized that social businesses, rather than charities, may be a better way to solve some of the world's problems. In his Nobel Prize interview Yunus explained the essence of conscious capitalism:

> Social businesses are businesses where you want to invest money to achieve a social objective... It's not a charity, it's not given and never seen back again... but I'm not doing it to make money for myself. I'm doing it to reach out to people, solve the social problems, solve an economic problem... I don't have to go around passing round a hat to collect money, because as a business it generates its own money and it continues.[3]

Today's conscious companies understand that ethical responsibility and environmental stewardship are not just goals; they're core components of a sustainable, engaging workplace culture. When employees feel part of a company making a positive impact, they're more productitve, loyal and motivated.

The rise of conscious capitalism

To dig deeper into the concept, I went right to the source – the founder of conscious capitalism, Raj Sisodia, bestselling author, international speaker and Professor at Tecnológico de Monterrey in Mexico, and the foremost leader in the modern conscious capitalism movement.

To Sisodia and his organization, a conscious company, or a firm of endearment as he's aptly named them, must serve the interests of all major stakeholders – customers, employees, investors, communities, suppliers and the environment – and is based on four tenets:

- Business can and should be done with a higher purpose that goes beyond profit.
- Businesses should seek to simultaneously deliver long-term benefits to all stakeholders instead of accepting trade-offs and focusing primarily on near-term returns to shareholders.
- Businesses should foster and promote conscious leaders who are driven by the firm's purpose and service to its people rather than power or self-enrichment. They lead by mentoring, motivating, developing and inspiring people rather than through a command-and-control, carrot-and-stick approach.
- Businesses should develop conscious cultures that embody qualities such as trust, accountability, caring, transparency, integrity, learning and empowerment.

Sisodia is a highly astute business professional, studying and teaching marketing since the mid 1980s. His book *Firms of Endearment: How world-class companies profit from passion and purpose* was one of the highest-praised business books of 2007. He has consulted with and taught programmes for global companies like AT&T, LG, Sprint, Volvo, IBM, Wal-Mart and McDonald's. He truly believes in harnessing the power of capitalism. To Sisodia, the conscious aspect of conscious capitalism enhances everything about the capitalism model. And he can back up this belief.

Through rigorous research of companies like Southwest Airlines, Starbucks and Whole Foods, Sisodia found that over a 15-year period conscious capitalist companies had investment returns of 1,646 per cent, whereas the S&P 500 companies showed only 157 per cent returns to their shareholders over the same timeframe. This finding alone would make the ears of any CEO perk up.

Yet, even in the face of this evidence, business leaders still demand to know why they should care about anything more than the single bottom line. After all, Isn't that what shareholders really want? what shareholders demand. Doing well as a business is a given, and it is certainly very important, but it is less obvious that doing good is just as critical, and just as attainable.

I asked Sisodia about the evolution of the conscious capitalist movement, and how the business leaders he consults with justify making the shift. 'This is something that all stakeholders care about,' he told me. 'People want businesses to have a positive impact, beyond making money. It impacts reputation, ability to attract customers; more and more customers care about things beyond just the price of the product.'

Do customers really care?

Most Gen Z and Millennials prefer to buy from ethical brands that truly care about people and the planet. According to a survey by OnePoll, 80 per cent are likely to base their purchases on a brand's mission or purpose.

In a first of its kind global study, research that analysed 8,000 consumers across eight countries (the United States, Canada, United Kingdom, France, China, India, Singapore, Malaysia) found that consumers are four to six times more likely to trust, buy, champion and protect companies with a strong purpose.[4] The results were striking: when consumers believed a brand had a strong purpose, they were four times more likely to purchase from the company, 4.5 times more likely to recommend it, 4.1 times more likely to trust it and six times more likely to defend it during public criticism.

So what are the benefits to companies shifting their mentality from profit-driven to purpose-driven? According to companies like 3M, Disney, REI, New Balance, BMW and IKEA, the benefit is simply success. These global brands, plus others in the same category, have consistently outperformed the S&P 500 by 14 times, and Good to Great Companies by 6 times over a period of 15 years (Figure 4.1).

So, now that we have the stats and figures to prove that conscious capitalism has real and tangible value, then shouldn't it give us just enough fuel to go out there and practise it?

Sisodia would say yes – with one caveat: 'You have to do the right things for the right reasons. CEOs who adopt the conscious capitalist methods solely for financial gains breed more cynicism and make customers and employees feel taken advantage of.'

FIGURE 4.1 Firms of endearment – cumulative returns 1998–2013

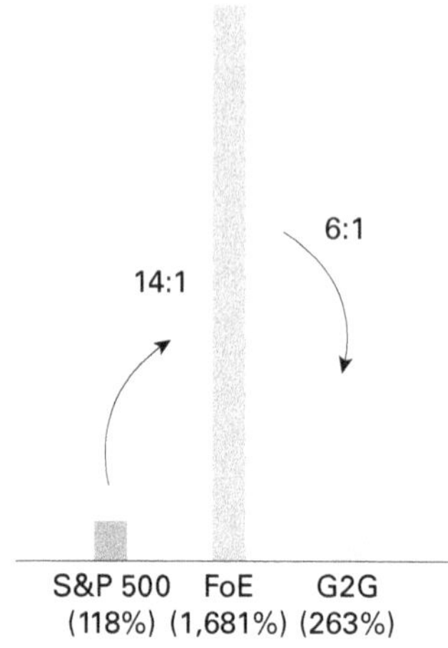

The firms of endearment (FoE) featured in this book have out-performed the S&P 500 by 14 times and good to great (G2G) companies by 6 times over a period of 15 years.

Cumulative performance	15 years	10 years	5 years	3 years
US FoE	1,681%	410%	151%	83%
International FoE	1,180%	512%	154%	47%
G2G companies	263%	176%	158%	222%
S&P 500	118%	107%	61%	57%

The talent attraction and retention benefit

The added bonus to building a business on the premise of a conscious strategy is that these same factors also help to attract and retain talent. Sisodia revealed to me that a conscious company has a better ability to attract employees who want to have a shared sense of purpose with their employer. He said: 'When you reconfigure the business this way, you tap into a lot of positive energy that's latent out there. People are capable of extraordinary levels of commitment and creativity and passion and engagement, but for the most part people have been shut down and are operating kind of at a minimal level, because they're not given conditions where all of that can be liberated.'

Like Sisodia, I have seen first-hand how compassionate and purposeful leadership transforms teams and businesses. Sisodia explained to me that many people in today's leadership positions owe their success to excelling in the traditional business ethos, which can make it difficult for them to pivot and see the value in not just the bottom line, but also 'the double bottom line', the measure of positive impact.

The leaders he consults with mostly reward, recognize and pay attention to the financial metrics, he said, 'unless they have had a personal awakening, unless they have some kind of transformative experience'. This is where the magic happens in Sisodia's line of work. Awakenings, epiphanies and 'aha' moments are the catalyst for change that can impact entire corporations. 'You cannot have a conscious business without a conscious leader, and you cannot be a conscious leader unless you are a conscious human being, so you have to work on yourself first.'

How can we shift from old patterns to new patterns?

These observations hit home for me: my personal and professional journeys have been littered with awakenings. Some came during an era of seeking growth and change. Some were uninvited. All were meaningful. Some of the most profound moments of positive shift came in the form of failures, losses and setbacks.

So I asked Sisodia if he has to wait for a leader to stumble upon their conscious capitalist epiphany, or if they can seek them out. He recounted stories of CEOs who had realizations at churches and weddings, after reading about the impact of climate change on the planet, or after having their children tell them they don't support the overly processed products their companies sell – like in the case of Indra Nooyi, CEO of Pepsi. Replicating the power of these real-life 'aha' moments is his 'greatest challenge', but Sisodia said it is possible, as long as leaders have 'some openness and some degree of questioning'.

According to Sisodia, even though traditional business methods are well-worn paths to success for many of his clients, there are also many of them contending with 'midlife and beyond'. He told me that this stage in life fosters self-examination and the desire for personal change and growth. He said these shifts in personal perspective are easily carried through into business practices.

Many CEOs, especially those who had already achieved significant success, faced unique reflections during the pandemic – some even experiencing those profound 'aha' moments about what truly matters. The crisis acted as a catalyst, prompting leaders to re-evaluate not only their personal lives but also their roles and responsibilities within their organizations. These moments of introspection, as Sisodia describes, can lead to a newfound emphasis on purpose and responsibility in leadership.

For example, Salesforce CEO Marc Benioff had a transformative shift during the pandemic. Benioff began reimagining Salesforce's role, not just as a technology company, but as a social force. He spearheaded initiatives to support communities and employees, like offering health and wellness benefits for remote work and implementing a 90-day customer payment deferral programme to ease financial burdens on clients.

Another instance is Ron Vachris, CEO of Costco, who had a defining moment when he stood up for DEI despite mounting pressure to abandon these practices. Risking backlash, Vachris publicly claimed that he believes equity and opportunity are both morally imperative and better for business. 'If these policies you see as offensive, I must tell you I am not prepared to change,' Vachris wrote in his communication to customers.

Some CEOs realized that their success was not merely about expanding profits but fostering a meaningful impact on people's lives: an ethos born from their own personal transformations and deep self-reflection during a time of collective crisis.

What it boils down to is that self-awareness is required for personal growth. Sisodia warns that leaders have to be 'very careful and thoughtful about the transition process'. He said, 'You cannot pull the plug suddenly on the old way.' Instead, Sisodia suggests 'ambidextrous energy' and 'what Richard Barrett calls a full spectrum consciousness': being able to simultaneously consider short- and long-term plans, never neglecting stakeholders and remembering to prioritize survival and revenue streams.

Like many business decisions, choosing a conscious capitalist path is both an investment and a risk, but with the right strategies and supports Sisodia says it's well worth it. 'You have to have a degree of faith,' he said, 'and believe that this is the right thing to do. You have to be able to say, "I want to do this even if it doesn't result in higher profits".' However, in Sisodia's many years of experience, 'It turns out it actually does benefit the business significantly.'

Here's how Costco, Chobani, Vital Farms, and Interface exemplify this approach and why it leads to happier workplaces.

COSTCO

When asked by John Leland in an interview for SmartBrief to define culture at Costco, CEO Jim Sinegal said, 'Do the right thing.' He went on to explain that this means, '1. Obey the law, 2. Take care of our customers, 3. Take care of our employees, 4. Respect our suppliers, and 5. Reward our shareholders, pretty much in that order.'[5]

This ethos has been integral to Costco's business model and its enduring success, which is why Costco Wholesale Corporation stands out as a model of conscious capitalism. They demonstrate that businesses can thrive financially while prioritizing the well-being of their stakeholders. At its core, Costco's philosophy centres around ethical practices, fair treatment of employees and a commitment to long-term sustainability.

A key part of this approach is Costco's focus on employee welfare. Unlike many companies in the retail sector, Costco pays its workers significantly above the industry average, with hourly wages recently surpassing $30. This investment in fair wages and comprehensive benefits has contributed to high employee satisfaction and low turnover rates, reinforcing Costco's commitment to treating its employees with respect and care.

Customer value is another hallmark of Costco's conscious capitalism. Known for its member-first approach, the company goes to great lengths to provide high-quality products at competitive prices, even during times of inflation and economic pressure. A famous example is Costco's decision to keep the price of its $1.50 hot-dog-and-soda combo unchanged for nearly forty years, a move that symbolizes its dedication to delivering value and maintaining customer trust.

Additionally, Costco builds strong relationships with suppliers, fostering mutually beneficial partnerships rooted in respect and ethical practices, which further contribute to its positive reputation and community goodwill.

Costco also takes environmental responsibility seriously, integrating sustainability into its business model. Through initiatives like reducing plastic packaging on products such as its rotisserie chicken, the company has managed to cut plastic waste significantly.

By improving packaging efficiency and investing in energy-saving measures across its stores, Costco addresses environmental concerns while still serving its customers effectively. These actions illustrate Costco's belief that prioritizing stakeholder interests – including employees, customers, suppliers, and the environment – leads to stronger, more resilient business practices.

CHOBANI

When it comes to conscious capitalism, Chobani, known for their yogurt brands, has been a standout example. At the National Retail Federation's 2023 event in New York City, discussions centred around AI, digital transformation and using technology to reduce turnover and enhance safety. But retail leaders also leaned into a deeper conversation on Chobani CEO Hamdi Ulukaya's philosophy of conscious capitalism, or stakeholder capitalism.

Hamdi Ulukaya, a Turkish immigrant, arrived in the US in 1994 and saw an opportunity to bring better-tasting yogurt to the American market. His journey transformed Chobani from a small yogurt start-up to a brand with over 20 per cent of the US yogurt market. As Chobani grew, so did its commitment to hiring and supporting underserved communities, including refugees in Utica, New York and Twin Falls, Idaho. Ulukaya hired translators, provided transportation and developed strong ties to refugee communities.

His mission to create a positive impact extends beyond Chobani through the Tent Partnership for Refugees, launched in 2016 to help other businesses employ refugees. This work has inspired companies like Amazon, Hilton and PepsiCo to hire refugees, proving that conscious capitalism isn't just good for communities; it's a powerful way to foster loyalty, boost productivity and increase brand appeal among socially-conscious consumers.[6]

VITAL FARMS

With nearly 200,000 businesses already integrating conscious capitalism practices, the goal is to grow that to 10 million conscious leaders, creating meaningful impact for all involved.

Vital Farms is part of that growing group. Led by CEO Russell Diez-Canseco, Vital Farms places humane animal treatment, fair wages and environmental sustainability at the core of its business. By offering above-standard wages, equity stakes and transparency in financials, Vital Farms has created a sense of community that goes beyond typical workplace dynamics. They even invite customers to trace their products back to specific farms, building trust with both employees and consumers.

When employees know their work is part of a transparent, ethical mission, it drives engagement. A recent report found that companies see a 52 per cent lower turnover among newer employees when they participate in corporate social responsibility programmes.[7] For Vital Farms, conscious capitalism translates directly into a happier, more cohesive team.

INTERFACE

Interface has taken its sustainability efforts a step further by committing to regenerative business practices. With innovations like carbon-negative carpet tiles and eco-friendly manufacturing processes, Interface's Climate Take Back initiative aims to restore ecosystems rather than merely preserving them. This forward-thinking approach has positioned Interface as a leader in sustainable manufacturing.

Employees at Interface feel proud to be part of a company actively working to improve the planet. A study published in *Sustainability* found that firms with strong corporate social responsibility performance experienced lower employee turnover, which in turn was associated with improved financial outcomes.[8] These companies show that conscious capitalism does more than just boost public perception – it creates a workplace where employees are deeply connected to their roles. When employees know their work has a positive impact, it transforms their job into a source of purpose and pride. Data consistently supports this: organizations with strong values-driven cultures see higher engagement, increased productivity and reduced turnover.[9]

Whether you have a life-changing moment that impacts your world view or you simply can't ignore the increasing insistence from employees and customers that your business should do the world more good, it's clear that conscious capitalism is the future. It not only creates a thriving double bottom line where profits meet purpose, the results are also worthwhile. The idea of 'us' and 'them' is thrown out and replaced with a shared vision that everyone wants to be part of.

HAPPINESS IN ACTION

- Grab your notebook and write down one area in your organization that demonstrates conscious capitalism. Explain how it embodies the concept described in this chapter. Do you think it helps or hinders your business, and why?
- Take an area of your organization that you would like to run with a conscious capitalist strategy. How would you action that? List the steps. Is it achievable? If not, go back to the list of steps to make it achievable. If it seems like something you could present to senior leadership or get started

on your own, go ahead and get started. Although it may seem like a daunting task, you will be amazed by how quickly others will step in to support you. And, in the end, we are responsible for the change we want to see. Also, I would love to hear how the strategies turn out so let me know how it goes and your case study might end up in my next book!

HAPPY LEARNING!

Read

- Mackey, J and Sisodia, R (2014) *Conscious Capitalism: Liberating the heroic spirit of business*, Highbridge Company
- Roddick, A (2000) *Business As Unusual*, Thorsons
- Sisodia, R, Wolfe, D and Sheth, J (2013) *Firms of Endearment: How world-class companies profit from passion and purpose*, 2nd edn, Harvard Business Review Publishing

Notes

1 A McWilliams. Corporate social responsibility: A theory of the firm perspective, *The Academy of Management Review*, 2001, 26, 117–27. 10.5465/AMR.2001.4011987.

2 The Nobel Prize. The Nobel Peace Prize 2006: Muhammad Yunus Facts, Nobel Prize, 2006. www.nobelprize.org/prizes/peace/2006/yunus/facts (archived at https://perma.cc/2QGJ-7WYT)

3 The Nobel Prize. Interview with 2006 Nobel Peace Laureate Muhammad Yunus, Nobel Prize, 2006. www.nobelprize.org/prizes/peace/2006/yunus/26087-interview-transcript-2006-3/ (archived at https://perma.cc/RT34-CWWX)

4 Zeno Group. 2020 Zeno strength of purpose study, Zeno Group Insights, 2020. www.zenogroup.com/insights/2020-zeno-strength-purpose (archived at https://perma.cc/999B-9235)

5 J Leland. Costco found the antidote to the ills of shareholder capitalism, SmartBrief, 2021. www.smartbrief.com/original/costco-found-the-antidote-to-the-ills-of-shareholder-capitalism (archived at https://perma.cc/4TCV-8FFH)

6 Ichor Strategies. Conscious capitalism as a core competency: A Chobani case study, Ideas and Insights, 2021. blog.ichorstrategies.com/ideas-insights-blog/conscious-capitalism-as-a-core-competency-a-chobani-case-study (archived at https://perma.cc/DNN2-7PRE)

7 Benevity. *Talent Retention Study*, 2022. https://cdn.bfldr.com/ZZ11QL2O/at/fxh6v7w5qkw3rk64hqsrs5/Talent_Retention_Study_2022.pdf (archived at https://perma.cc/NW75-QZX5)

8 C-H Chang et al. Employee satisfaction, corporate social responsibility and financial performance, *Sustainability*, 2021, 13 (18), 9996. doi.org/10.3390/su13189996 (archived at https://perma.cc/X99A-ZZ52)

9 Great Place to Work. How great company culture increases business profitability, Great Place to Work, 2021, blog.greatplacetowork.ie/blog/how-great-company-culture-increases-business-profitability (archived at https://perma.cc/4X6Y-YAWX)

5

The happiness disruptors

Happiness might be one of the oldest expressions of emotion in the history of human evolution, but when it comes to happiness at work many executives still assume it's all 'chanting and crystals'. Essentially, it's 'unscientific'.

Some of you may still be waiting for that one piece of evidence that will concretely convince you of the importance of unlocking happiness at work. The piece of evidence that will enable you to embrace, both rationally and emotionally, the concepts, science and research I've presented, despite any previous indoctrinated beliefs.

So, my job over the latter half of the book will be to coalesce the content so you can think about how to integrate a happiness strategy within your organizations. But I also want to open up the lid on some of those areas of our business that can cause stress. What is most enlightening about these happiness disruptors is that they are just common business practices. They offer numerous benefits but they can also be hindrances to our happiness.

In this chapter I will share the common mistakes we make when we onboard new strategies, tools and tactics, even the ones that seemingly make perfect sense. By identifying which happiness disruptors are the most prevalent and misunderstood, we can help our employees engage with them in a healthy and more effective way.

The technology explosion

Some of you may be quick to ask, how is technology stressful? And, you would be fair in asking that question. There are many examples of how technology improves our lives, a few of which I will share in the coming pages. However, with the increased proliferation of technology that is flowing between work and life, we can also feel like we're always turned on and tuned in. There are pros and cons to the increase in connectivity over the last decade. However, the negative consequences of overdosing on technology are worth taking a closer look at.

Let's explore a few of these hidden happiness disruptors.

Disadvantages of technology in the workplace

As I mentioned earlier, technology can feel all-encompassing. Although there has been considerable discussion about whether internet addiction should be categorized as a diagnosis in the fifth edition of the *Diagnostic and Statistical Manual of Mental Disorders* (DSM-5), it still hasn't been included. However, internet gaming disorder has been identified in Section III of the DSM-5 as a condition warranting more clinical research and experience before it might be considered for inclusion in the main book as a formal disorder.[1]

Some psychiatrists have argued that internet addiction shows the features of excessive use, withdrawal phenomena, tolerance and negative repercussions that characterize many substance use disorders. According to Dr Vivek Murthy, the US General Surgeon, excessive use of social media can disrupt important healthy behaviours. Persistent exposure to social media can overstimulate the brain's reward centre and, when the stimulation becomes excessive, can trigger pathways comparable to addiction.[2]

This is obviously a fairly bleak look at the negative consequences of excessive use of technology in our daily lives. Although this is something to be aware of, technology is also playing out in less dramatic ways that still cause stress for our employees. Here are some examples of where we need to focus our attention:

- **Decreased creativity:** Since most tasks are automated by technology it can stifle creative ways to problem solve or think innovatively about our work. As we've learned from earlier chapters, this can build up boredom, a state that can act like kryptonite on engagement.
- **Negative impact on relationships:** When we are over-using digital communication, face-to-face interactions are reduced. And interpersonal communications are extremely important in building happier and more creative/innovative cultures. When individuals get the chance to collide and collaborate, or even share non-work-related information, this builds community. Community is one of the most essential aspects of workplace retention strategies. The ability to rely strictly on technology for

communication can give people a way of avoiding the fostering of healthy friendships.

- **Disruption of our sleep patterns:** This adversely impacts our mood and our problem-solving skills.
- **Insecurity:** Employees who are inexperienced with technology can feel obsolete and unsure of their skills. This insecurity can lead to disengagement and fear of job loss. Today, one in two workers fear becoming obsolete due to the mass adoption of AI.

We can see that digital communication may be dumbing down our conversation abilities and that we're losing the ability to make friends without hiding behind the technology mask. In her bestselling book, *Alone Together*, MIT Professor and Psychologist Sherry Turkle says she believes we're 'getting a sense of connection without the demands of intimacy and the responsibilities of intimacy'.[3]

But Nancy Baym, Principal Researcher at Microsoft Research, doesn't share these concerns. In an NPR radio interview with Iris Adler, Nancy seemed to hold the opposing belief, that digital communications augment relationships instead. She says every new technology raises the fear that we will lose or lessen our human connections, but that we eventually figure out how to adapt.[4]

Following this stream of thought, let's now examine some of the positives of technology. Since technology isn't going anywhere and it's only going to become more significant to our success as leaders, we need to come up with new ways to increase flourishing in partnership with technology. To help our people avoid happiness hazards in their work experiences we'll need to reduce some of the negative impacts from the overuse of technology described above.

How technology improves our happiness in the workplace

With enhanced and more affordable technologies coming into the workplace, most employers now accept their daily use in the office. Like Nancy Baym mentions, in many ways technology has augmented our work life.[5] We have the capacity to perform tasks faster and with greater efficiency, and we've reduced the amount of administrative work that tends to dissipate our brain's energy.

Some people remember what it was like before technology conducted much of everyday life, while others don't understand how we could function without it. Its influence is felt on several different levels in our personal lives, our professional lives, with our kids at school – basically at most intersections of our life. Technology has revolutionized our world and, as such, businesses are realizing that in order to remain competitive, they too have to build enhanced technology strategies in the workplace. Everything from 'bring your own device' (BYOD) rather than providing computers and laptops, to 'bring your own AI' (BYOIA) where AI apps like ChatGPT have become ubiquitous. Employers are encouraging social media breaks to check out happy cat videos for a mood boost. Although there are risks to an 'anything goes' attitude to technology in the workplace, it seems to be the norm today.

According to PEW Research, 34 per cent of workers use social media at work to take a mental break from their job. Allowing employees to take brief social media breaks can serve as mental refreshers as long as the content is positive.[6]

And consider that the University of Melbourne's Professor Brent Coker found 70 per cent of the people who were allowed to browse the internet for up to 20 per cent of their day increased their overall productivity by 9 per cent. Coker notes, 'Short and unobtrusive breaks, such as a quick surf of the internet, enables the mind to reset itself, leading to a higher total net concentration for a day's work, and as a result, increased productivity'.[7]

And there are other benefits to using technology at work:

- **Global-mindedness:** When we bridge communication across cultures and in other languages, we build up our cognitive empathy, which plays out inside our internal teams.
- **Enhanced connections:** Social media collaboration tools in the workplace can provide warmth unfelt in mass email. It also scales and flattens communication between managers and employees.
- **Flexibility:** Obviously speed is crucial to today's rapidly moving, highly competitive business world. Technology is hugely influential in transferring communication in a controlled and efficient way. Organizations that incorporate the newest technology are better able to meet the needs of their clients because when information is portable, we can live and work in a world on the go. This is critical for me as a parent. I have the flexibility to be home if there is a sick child home from school. I don't have to forgo dinner with my family because of a long commute. I can take breaks during the day that consider the unpaid labour part of life that can lead to burnout if unwieldy. When we authentically care about the work–life continuum the results are retention, loyalty and engagement.

And what has been the response to organizations that are redesigning work processes by changing the way they handle information technology (IT) management, sales and marketing, human resources and customer service? In a survey by Avanade that looked at the trends surrounding the use of personal computing technologies in the enterprise space, they found that, amongst companies that changed at least one business process to adapt to the increased use of mobile devices, the results had been overwhelmingly positive:

- 73 per cent more likely to report improved sales.
- 54 per cent more likely to report increased profits.
- 58 per cent more likely to report improvement in bringing products and services to market.

Avanade calls this adaptive approach to the changing work environment 'work redesigned'. It means a more inclusive, creative and collaborative workplace. It means greater mobility and flexibility. It also means happier employees – the survey found that companies that embrace this approach were 37 per cent more likely to report improved employee satisfaction.[8]

How can we take the lessons learned above, and figure out a way to diminish the negative impacts of the over-use of technology but bridge them with healthier approaches to IT strategies? And what is the benefit to us as leaders for making that investment of time, resources and budget?

My preference is a blend of both the online and analogue worlds for increased well-being. We can now look to technology to remind us that it's time to get up and move. Yes, it may seem ridiculous that technology has to coax us, but how is that any different than a therapist guiding us to make healthier decisions regarding our mental health, or our personal trainer pushing us to do five more sit-ups than we did the last time we worked out?

I sat down with Amy Blankson, digital well-being strategist, cofounder of the Digital Well-being Institute and author of *The Future of Happiness*, to discuss how technology and happiness can sustainably align. Her book focuses on how to not just survive but actually thrive in the digital age.

Amy expressed a similar belief that technology is ever-present in our lives and – especially with the rise of AI adoption – is not going away. So, we need to imagine new ways to use it as a tool for shaping a happier life. Amy shared with me that 'by rethinking when, where, why and how we use technology, not only are we able to influence our own well-being, but we're also able to help to actively shape the future of our communities'. She also said:

'For years, we have bought into the idea that technology is supposed to help us become more productive, so that we can use more of our free time to do the things that make us happy. Companies are finding that just because they invest in new tech and introduce it to their workforce, that doesn't mean the tech will be integrated or even appreciated. When new innovation doesn't jive with how people actually work on a day-to-day basis, tech can actually decrease productivity and happiness.'

I asked Blankson where technology overwhelm is coming from and how we can tackle it. She shared some key insights from her latest LinkedIn Learning course, Balancing AI Adoption and Digital Well-being.

First, techno-stress is a particular kind of stress induced by the rapid adoption of new technologies which, Blankson says, is 'giving way to fatigue, irritability, a reduction in job satisfaction, and lower productivity'.

The rapid nature of adopting new AI technology is placing even more stress on a stressed-out workforce. She describes five forms of techno-stress to look for in your team members. They are:

- Techno-overload: A feeling of not keeping up with information.
- Techno-complexity: Overwhelm from using complex AI tools.
- Techno-insecurity: Mistrust of AI due to inaccuracy and lack of regulation.
- Techno-uncertainty: Fear of job replacement by AI.
- Techno-invasion: The feeling that AI is taking over and humans are helpless to do anything about it.

So as leaders, how can we fix it?

Validating that it's real and we need to address techno-stress, and being able to label what specific type of techno-stress we're facing, is the first step, as Blankson highlights.

After we recognize the signs, Blankson says we should 'Throttle the flow. Cut back on the source of overwhelm. You don't have to go cold turkey. But rather cut back 5–10 per cent'.

Now take your digital pulse. On her website, www.digitalwellnessinstitute.com (archived at https://perma.cc/9VM4-5GPP), Blankson has set up a free pulse survey, the Digital Flourishing Model, to help people check in with themselves and rebalance the eight digital domains of their life.

Amy and I agree that we can use technology to build healthier habits. If technology can act as a reminder to get us to a meeting on time, why can't it act as a reminder to stretch, or calm our minds for two minutes, or build up our gratitude and empathy?

And technology can help our employees thrive, not just survive, at work. Technology can often bridge the divide between the online and offline world. For example:

- It can support the use of workplace social collaboration tools that enhance relationship-building and encourage taking conversations offline.
- Wearables, like fitness activity trackers for example, can suggest increasing steps, taking walking meetings, or even just getting up and stepping away from desks after long periods of sitting.
- Mindfulness apps will nudge you offline to take ten minutes of quiet meditation.
- Encourage some healthy 'time apart' from devices – this is a great suggestion for your employees. Maybe it's a 'no email at lunch' rule or making sure digital communication doesn't happen after or before certain hours of the day.
- Make sure automation isn't destroying creativity. Find ways for employees who rely heavily on technology to explore creative outlets. Perhaps make break time an opportunity to explore and stimulate inspiration.
- Finally, have trust. Watching over employees like hawks, ensuring they are limiting their use of technology only serves to demotivate employees. Happiness is built on trust; and allowing your employees to make decisions around appropriate use of technology is necessary to build a culture of openness. To micro manage the distraction of technology is itself a distraction. Plus, it won't play out well with the next generation of Gen Z hires and beyond where digital life is just that... life.

Technology can cause our employees stress, so we need to recognize this and respond. It can also be a valuable tool that provides helpful support in a variety of areas, so considering technology in our happiness strategies is vital to a flourishing culture.

The pitfalls of professional development

Another area that is causing us happiness disruption can be found in the lack of learning and personal/professional development (PD) inside our organizations today. We continue to enhance our efforts to provide PD to our leadership and identify high performers who are called out as people to retain at all costs. Although we shouldn't ignore their value to the greater success of the organization, we are missing a pretty wide swathe of people who could benefit greatly from additional learning, education and ongoing training.

We also focus too much on building on the existing skills of our employees. We all understand how and why it's necessary to maintain a designation as a chartered professional accountant through so many hours of continuing education. Or keeping up human resources, legal professional credits or medical designates through training and certifications. But, why don't we invest more to increase resiliency, mindfulness, empathy, gratitude – overall emotional intelligence?

In the first edition I cited a 2010 study, *The Business Case for Emotional Intelligence*, which found that when asked 'What are the top issues you face at work?' leaders identified 76 per cent on the people/relational side, and only 24 per cent on the finance/technical side. Among these 135 respondents, a massive 89 per cent identify emotional quotient (EQ) as 'highly important' or 'essential' to meeting their organizations' top challenges.[9]

Thirteen years later and guess what? Either I can predict the future or this is an evergreen need that we must consider – emotional intelligence is a key skill if you want to be a high-performing company.

According to the 2023 World Economic Forum *Future of Jobs* report, 'analytical thinking' is considered to be a core skill by more companies than any other skill. 'Another cognitive skill, creative thinking, ranks second, ahead of three self-efficacy skills – resilience, flexibility and agility; motivation and self-awareness; and curiosity and lifelong learning – in recognition of the importance of workers' ability to adapt to disrupted workplaces.'[10]

The WEF report also claims 'dependability and attention to detail ranks seventh, behind technological literacy'. And the core skills top 10 is completed by two attitudes relating to working with others – empathy and active listening, and leadership and social influence.

This is noteworthy. 'Management skills, engagement skills, technology skills, ethics and physical abilities are generally considered to be less important than cognition, self-efficacy, and working with others.'

Let's take this into the real world and how EQ training along with technical training could be beneficial.

Take a front-facing customer service agent working at a car dealership, for example. They've been handling a deluge of calls about a safety issue with a specific car part. Wouldn't it be helpful if they'd spent the last six weeks going through empathy training to bridge a relationship faster, solve the issue and retain the relationship?

Or what about a sales professional trying to stay hopeful after hearing the word 'no' more times than they can count? Wouldn't resiliency training help him to jump back on another call faster or be able to turn those challenging conversations around?

How about educators? Let's imagine a teacher who year after year teaches fourth grade. She loves it, but rarely does she find out whether that challenging year with a student had any positive impact on their future. Wouldn't it be fantastic if they were trained in optimism so they could believe their work is meaningful even if they may never know how their efforts pay off?

Although we've only examined a few very specific examples of how emotional intelligence training can enhance our business outcomes, I'm optimistic that you can imagine many scenarios of your own where this kind of training could be helpful.

The continuing education deficit

Corporate learning budgets are often one of the first areas to face cuts during economic downturns or periods of financial uncertainty. This happens for several reasons, many tied to immediate cost-control strategies and shifting organizational priorities.

According to a 2022 study, 75 per cent of senior HR leaders believe economic uncertainty is impacting their company's learning and development (L&D) strategy, with many looking to cut training costs as a result.[11]

Recently, Meta and other tech giants reduced their L&D budgets, choosing to pivot resources towards immediate revenue-generating activities. Similarly, in sectors hit by post-pandemic slowdowns, like retail and hospitality, companies have slashed learning budgets to conserve resources for core operational needs.[12] These cuts in corporate learning budgets come at a time when upskilling is critical, which is ironic but demonstrates the delicate balance companies must strike between long-term growth and short-term survival. The study also showed that two-thirds of workers were more likely to choose a role with a career progression plan over an identical job with a higher salary. And the 'majority of employees say L&D is a "vital" factor in choosing an employer, with 83 per cent of employees surveyed claiming that professional development at their workplace made them feel more "valued"'.

Other research finds that dissatisfaction with employee development efforts often led to early exits for young high-performers.[13]

How learning equals loyalty

Although it can be expensive, it is necessary to build in a culture of learning as soon as someone joins your company. It pays off in a myriad of valuable ways.

Some of the most innovative enterprise companies in the world are described as high-impact learning organizations (HILOs), which means they are better at skills development and talent development than other organizations in this area.

In his foundation study, Josh Bersin and his team found that these HILOs tend to significantly outperform their peers in several areas:

- They are 32 per cent more likely to be first to market.
- They have 37 per cent greater employee productivity.
- They have a 34 per cent better response to customer needs.
- They have a 26 per cent greater ability to deliver quality products.
- They are 58 per cent more likely to have skills to meet future demand.
- They are 17 per cent more likely to be market share leaders.[14]

Today, according to *The Definitive Guide to Learning: Growth in the flow of work*, the largest and latest research study produced by the Josh Bersin Company, 'effective learning and development (L&D) departments are no longer training functions – they're growth functions'. Bersin shared these key findings:

- 78 per cent of companies regard L&D as a top C-suite priority, but 4 out of 5 organizations are lagging in every L&D area.
- Most organizations consider learning in the flow of work the zenith of learning outcomes, yet, only 12 per cent do it effectively.
- The number one most impactful L&D practice today is to create extensive career growth options.
- Only 17 per cent of organizations create extensive opportunities for career growth.[15]

The Bersin team found that the number one biggest driver of business growth and impact on business outcomes is a result of learning and development programmes that focus on career management (developing career pathways, creating career coaches, giving people self-service career tools).

'As many have heard me talk about, there's too much noise about skills as the currency of success,' Bersin says. 'Yes, we each need granular skills to do our jobs. But we can't really use these skills, hone them, or apply them unless we have context, experiences, mentoring, and wisdom. This "wisdom" comes through growth: taking a stretch assignment, working on a new project, or meeting someone who can help you fill in the gaps.'[16]

He goes on to explain, 'There is no point going to training if you don't build the right skills; there's no point building a skill if you can't apply it on the job; and there's no point creating a capability unless it can help you grow, expand, and do new things. That's what's going on – we're stretching the role of L&D to focus on growth, not just learning.'

What this reinforces is an urgent need to engage people's purpose and focus on developing EQ and wisdom for better business outcomes. The skills required the most these days are not technical but cognitive skills that help us to better connect to our work and the stakeholders we serve.

One of my favourite pieces about how to build a learning culture originates from Paul Schoemaker, Research Director at Wharton's Mack Institute. He talked about making learning a daily habit. He believes that our business-building habits are just like riding a bike – practice makes perfect. Schoemaker believes that since learning is contagious, 'the behavior of the boss becomes critical'.[17]

He emphasized that leaders should be the 'focal point as well as champions for learning because they are the most well positioned to shine a spotlight on success as well as failure'. This is a key attribute of innovative companies because they aren't constantly de-risking their decisions. Mistakes are just hidden opportunities for learning.

What I appreciate about Schoemaker's philosophy is this iterative approach to learning. The concept of 'failing forward' is part of my everyday vernacular. It's served me well over the years as I push myself to take risks and put myself out there on stages all over the world. I was one of those people who would have chosen a root canal over public speaking. But, when you're working with organizations that have over one million employees, you aren't often in one-on-ones. I had to get comfortable being in front of large audiences. I came to realize three things:

1 Everyone wants you to do well up there on stage – view them as your cheerleaders.

2 If you know your topic, you'll be fine. Mastery moderates imposter syndrome.
3 Picturing the audience naked is weird.

It's also critical to be prepared. If you want your people to feel prepared, they need to get in a habit of practice and be OK with failing forward.

Schoemaker offers a few quick tips for creating an environment that rewards enquiry and learning:

- Conduct pre-decision and post mortem debriefs to extract insights.
- Build the necessary discipline to look at failure as well as success.
- Internalize mistakes and lessons learned, and then apply them broadly.
- Stop initiatives that are not producing as expected; know when to pull the plug.
- Conduct annual learning audits where prized projects can be challenged.

There are obvious benefits to building a culture of learning. Not only does it encourage employees and organizations to develop knowledge and competence but also it inspires passionate and engaged thought – something that creates enthusiasm and drive in most people involved in any project. Our brains yearn for constant learning as it elevates us, it opens opportunities to innovate and rapidly as well as continuously transform.

What we've learned from the above is that a culture of learning can:

- increase efficiency, productivity and profit
- increase employee satisfaction and decreased turnover
- improve mindset among employees
- develop a sense of ownership and accountability
- ease in succession/transition/change management

My hot take on what hot desks represent

Another hidden stressor these days for everyone – leaders and their employees – can be found in the shifting experience of 'where' we work. For those employees who are most content with predictable and routine workplace environments, moving impacts psychological safety, crucial to engagement and happiness.

After working remotely in the pandemic, it shifted workers' mind-sets about the office and what it represents. Spaces have also shifted. For those returning to in-person it can feel jarring. Some employees who had a specific space to return to are now grabbing any space they can find. They also feel that a return to office is arbitrary as they come in to replicate what they could be doing at home.

Part of the stress also ties back to a sense of agency and control of our work environment. You might find your cat jumping across your keyboard is a distraction – but at least it's a known risk. At the office human interactions are highly variable. It can be a pleasant experience. It can also be stressful.

According to a survey conducted by the Industrial Society entitled *The State of the Office*, most of us feel we do not have enough control over our working environment.[18] And a recent Korn Ferry article titled 'Hot-desking: Not so hot with employees' claims that firms wanted to get more workers back in the office, but reduce office-space expenses. These firms believed 'it would create social, flexible workspaces for employees and save millions of dollars'.[19]

What happened is a doubling of 'hot desks' – where employees do not have assigned desks, instead they choose available workstations daily based on their needs. Yet research finds that employees strongly dislike the practice. It makes sense. We now have a comparison that we didn't otherwise have pre-pandemic. The question facing leaders today is, 'Why would workers want to come into the office for setups that are less comfortable than those at home?'

In Research: How coworking spaces impact employee well-being published by *Harvard Business Review*, the authors share that employees who preferred working remotely, over half were trying to avoid 'unwanted interactions with colleagues.'[20]

In Korn Ferry's This Week in Leadership, Mark Royal, PhD and Senior Client Partner for Korn Ferry suggests that giving certainty about where people will work each day is a simple stress-mitigation tactic. 'Avoid uncertainties, like "Where am I going to sit today?" and "Will I have what I need?",' he says. Making sure that employees have the right chairs, lighting, and monitor setups can also go a long way.[21]

For some, the issue lies in the requirement for their role to have privacy and quiet or the necessity to be very, very loud. From sound editors and developers to frontline sales teams, one job might require absolute quiet and the other a room where they can ring a gong if they so prefer.

For others, it is part of their genetic makeup. Introverts, for example. According to Susan Cain, author of *'Quiet: The power of introverts in a world that can't stop talking'*, introverts are people who 'recharge' by spending time alone. They need periods of solitude in order to thrive, be more creative and more productive.[22]

Although a desk isn't the only way for someone to find personal space, it is imperative for employers to know that introverts are known to be easily stimulated and thus easily tired out by prolonged interactions with people. And according to Glori Surban in her article, 'How to manage introverted employees in the workplace', open-space offices can be challenging. Although teamwork is valuable, introverts flourish when they work independently. By asking introverts to hot desk, you run the risk of having one group constantly moving towards spaces that are tucked away without the risk of interruption and a flood of people who are looking for distractions and noise that will be drawn to open areas. This is sure to be detrimental to everyone's creative process.[23]

The main takeaway from the topic of hot-desking is much more macro than decoding whether this is something that is good or bad for your team. It's about agency and feeling like someone is listening to your needs. It could be any trend that we decide to test – the key here is that we need to ask first. Assessing whether something is going to work has to be based on solid data and evidence that describes how the character of your organization will react to such a sweeping change.

The happiness disruptor isn't as micro as asking someone to start hot-desking, the happiness disruptor happens when we stop asking or caring how our employees feel about the changes ahead. And if we are going to make changes despite what we learn, be prepared for varying degrees of unhappiness within your teams.

To recap: whether it's leading your teams through change, or deciding how to develop an IT strategy that promotes well-being, or creating a contagious culture of learning that proliferates across your entire organization, or making changes to the workspace, ensure that individuals are looped into the process.

There is no doubt that it requires work. A huge amount of effort and intention goes into solving these big problems. But along with a decision to tackle the biggest challenges comes the opportunity to create a happiness domino effect that translates into using EQ to solve problems in other parts of the organization. It just takes one push, and the rest of the dominoes fall into place.

In the next chapter we'll dig into how work and happiness in the workplace is personal. And why we need bespoke happiness strategies for a changing workforce persona. We'll discuss more effective engagement strategies that scale to suit the unique needs of each individual rather than creating blanket strategies that fail. I look forward to meeting you again in the next chapter after you spend some time on the tactical applications below.

HAPPINESS IN ACTION

Questions and answers

- Describe the culture of learning at your organization.
- Is there a budget allocated for some or all employees with regards to learning initiatives?
- How would you improve your investment in learning if you have an increase in budget of 5 per cent?
- How about 25 per cent?
- Do you invest time in your own professional development?
- If you could spend more time developing yourself personally, where would you invest your time?
- If you could spend more time developing yourself professionally, where would you invest your time?

Try it on for size

- Spend two weeks without a desk and keep a journal outlining how it feels to live without a space. Include as much detail as possible and share back with your team the feedback from your experiment.
- Ask volunteers to do the same for two weeks and get their feedback.
- If there is another initiative that you're looking at testing, tweak the experiment so you are the first guinea pig. By testing it first, this will give you an empathetic filter of which will help guide the experience for others.

HAPPY LEARNING!

Read

- Bersin, J (2004) *The Blended Learning Book: Best practices, proven methodologies, and lessons learned*, Pfeffer
- Cain, S (2012) *Quiet: The power of introverts in a world that can't stop talking*, Crown Publishers
- Schoemaker, P (2011) *Brilliant Mistakes: Finding success on the far side of failure*, Wharton Digital Press
- Seligman, M (2011) *Flourish: A visionary understanding of happiness and well-being*, Nicholas Brealey Publishing

Notes

1 American Psychiatric Association. What is internet gaming disorder? American Psychiatric Association, nd. https://www.psychiatry.org/patients-families/internet-gaming (archived at https://perma.cc/8E2M-XEJY)

2 Yale Medicine. Social media and teen mental health: A parent's guide, Yale Medicine, 2023. www.yalemedicine.org/news/social-media-teen-mental-health-a-parents-guide (archived at https://perma.cc/R2DF-2W5J)

3 S Turkle (2011). *Alone Together: Why we expect more from technology and less from each other*, Basic Books.

4 WBUR. How our digital devices are affecting our personal relationships, WBUR, 2013. www.wbur.org/news/2013/01/17/digital-lives-i (archived at https://perma.cc/PV3K-CQPH)

5 WBUR. How our digital devices are affecting our personal relationships, WBUR, 2013. www.wbur.org/news/2013/01/17/digital-lives-i (archived at https://perma.cc/PV3K-CQPH)

6 A Perrin. Social media and the workplace, Pew Research Center, 2016. www.pewresearch.org/internet/2016/06/22/social-media-and-the-workplace (archived at https://perma.cc/6HAL-BREB)

7 B Coker. Freedom to surf: The positive effects of workplace internet leisure browsing, *New Technology, Work and Employment*, 2011, 26. 10.1111/j.1468-005X.2011.00272.x

8 E Saviz. Consumerization of IT, Forbes, 2012. www.forbes.com/sites/ciocentral/2012/02/20/consumerization-of-it-getting-beyond-the-myths/ (archived at https://perma.cc/R2UJ-HHD2)

9 J Freedman. *The Business Case for Emotional Intelligence*, Six Seconds, 2010. exceptionalhorizons.com/pdfs/EQ_Business_Case_2010-6-seconds.pdf (archived at https://perma.cc/F2HD-9C9C)

10 World Economic Forum. *The Future of Jobs Report 2023*, World Economic Forum, 2023. https://www.weforum.org/publications/the-future-of-jobs-report-2023 (archived at https://perma.cc/5TKN-LYDY)

11 ExecOnline. Winning with strategic leadership development during economic uncertainty, *ExecOnline*, 2022. www.execonline.com/winning-with-strategic-leadership-development-during-economic-uncertainty (archived at https://perma.cc/5GTV-7AAD)

12 K Wagner. Meta to cut headcount for first time, slash budgets across teams, Bloomberg, 2022. finance.yahoo.com/news/meta-announces-hiring-freeze-warns-183143714.html (archived at https://perma.cc/CF7W-AZMT)

13 Exude, Inc. Why employee development is important and can cost you talent, Exude, 2024. exudehc.com/blog/why-employee-development-is-important-and-can-cost-you-talent (archived at https://perma.cc/N74X-2TTC)

14 J Bersin. The new best-practices of a high-impact learning organization, Josh Bersin, 2012. joshbersin.com/2012/09/the-new-best-practices-of-a-high-impact-learning-organization (archived at https://perma.cc/7AYF-6HMF)

15 J Bersin. *The Definitive Guide to Learning: Growth in the flow of work*. Josh Bersin, 2022. joshbersin.com/definitive-guide-to-learning (archived at https://perma.cc/4VP2-VYDP)

16 J Bersin. *The Definitive Guide to Learning: Growth in the flow of work*. Josh Bersin, 2022. joshbersin.com/definitive-guide-to-learning (archived at https://perma.cc/4VP2-VYDP)

17 P Schoemaker. How to link strategic vision to core capabilities, *Strategy & Leadership*, 1992, 20 (5), 56–64.

18 The Industrial Society (2002) *The State of the Office: The politics and geography of working space*, The Industrial Society.

19 Korn Ferry. Hot-desking: Not so hot with employees, *Korn Ferry*, 2023. www.kornferry.com/insights/this-week-in-leadership/hot-desking-not-so-hot-with-employees (archived at https://perma.cc/SE24-264B)

20 C Hadley et al. Research: How coworking spaces impact employee wellbeing, *Harvard Business Review*, 2023. hbr.org/2023/02/research-how-coworking-spaces-impact-employee-wellbeing

21 Korn Ferry. Hot-desking: Not so hot with employees, *Korn Ferry*, 2023. www.kornferry.com/insights/this-week-in-leadership/hot-desking-not-so-hot-with-employees (archived at https://perma.cc/SE24-264B)

22 S Cain (2012) *Quiet: The power of introverts in a world that can't stop talking*, Crown Publishers.

23 G Surban. How to manage introverted employees in the workplace, *The People Management*, 2023. thepeoplemanagement.com/how-to-manage-introvert-employees-in-the-workplace-aparna-sharma-senior-hr-professional-certified-corporate-director-i-editors-collection (archived at https://perma.cc/6X9R-XMSV)

6

Engaging the whole person

The average person spends over 90,000 hours at work over their lifetime.[1] But, arguably, since the conception of work, we've made an exhaustive effort to keep our work lives and our home lives separate. In the past there was a solid rationale for bifurcating these two existences. Less than a century ago, rural farming was still an important occupation and the working class was often divided according to socioeconomic status, with the wealthiest making up only a small percentage of the total labour force. Most of the working class struggled to make a decent living in factories, shipyards and farming communities. Men, women and children worked in factories, often receiving pay that was not commensurate with their labour.

But overall, for many, work was just another harsh and intolerable day to endure. Unfortunately, despite the gains in labour protections and safer working conditions, Gallup finds that 77 per cent of the global workforce remains disengaged[2] and Mercer's 2024 workforce trends report claims that 83 per cent are at risk of burning out this year.[3]

A series of studies on work related to healthiness over time (that took place over the span of eight decades) continues to bolster the argument that high engagement at work increases health, well-being and longevity. [4]

One of those studies draws on the findings from an unprecedented study of 1,528 high-potential children followed from the early 1920s until their deaths. 'The longevity project: Surprising discoveries for health and long life from the landmark eight-decade study' claims that 'workers who advanced in their careers and took on more responsibility were also more likely to live long, healthy lives'. Co-author Howard S. Friedman, a Psychologist at the University of California, Riverside, notes, 'If you want to improve your health, you shouldn't just go on a joyride, but get involved in meaningful, productive kinds of things'.[5]

How work makes us feel alive... and keeps us alive, too

So, if work is supposed to be so good for us, why is it still causing so much stress? And, what is in the secret sauce of people who love their jobs?

For some, it's the meaning they draw from the work. For others, it's the sense of accomplishment from our work-related activities. The word 'accomplishment' is actually quite vital to this statement. It happens to be represented by the A in PERMA, Martin Seligman's happiness model that suggests having a regular sense of accomplishment is a key driver of lifelong flourishing and well-being.

In a world of work where there is such a blurring of lines between our personal and professional selves it's even more important to focus on happiness in general – not bifurcated between work and life.

And it's why I strongly dislike the term work/life balance, despite how ubiquitous this term has become. This concept was intended to advance happiness at work and yet has radically hindered it. Work/life balance was a term born out of the United Kingdom in the 1970s and is defined as 'a comfortable state of equilibrium achieved between an employee's primary priorities of their employment position and their private lifestyle'.[6] Work/life balance wasn't even uttered in the United States until the mid 1980s and it still took another two decades before it became common vernacular in the workplace and in popular media.

For some time now, this shift has been extremely puzzling and challenging for employers. Both employees and employers were quite content with work being a place at which to invest forty years and then retire. You had loyalty on both sides, and a very stable, constant reliability attached to the concept of work.

But times change.

It became apparent that we needed to solve the problem of imbalance with the overworked, overstressed workforce who were missing crucial time with family, relationships and the outside world of work. So, the work/life balance theory grew in popularity. It certainly sounded nice. Harmonious. Equitable. Healthy.

Unfortunately, words are not actions. And, after decades of research, we've witnessed how this balancing act has slowly evolved into a high-wire performance, impossible to sustain and sadly, without any nets in sight. According to Anne Perschel, in a 2010 edition of *Global Business and Organizational Excellence*:

> the notion of work as separate from life is a relatively new paradigm that is neither healthy nor productive… the goal of work/life balance being one such example. In seeking the formula for the perfect way to divide our time and energy between work and life, we strive for the near impossible, and then feel guilty. We question what we are doing wrong such that 'balance' continues to elude us.[7]

When something is good in theory but not in practice and if we can't rely on the policies which we are building, then all of us have to recognize that it will never be successful. So, perhaps, instead of continuing to attempt new ways to iterate on an old model, it's time to build a new one. What if we asked ourselves this – can work and life be allies not enemies? Rather than bifurcate, can they flow together instead?

One of the main reasons it doesn't work is that what happens in our personal lives is interconnected with our professional lives. It's not like the Apple TV series, *Severance*, which is built on a highly ironic and relatable storyline about a company that uses a neural implant to keep employees' memories between work and life completely separated in the brain.

Much to the dismay of some employers, employees have long memories. So, it's no wonder they resist RTO mandates when they've felt the benefits of being able to work flexibly and policies like Return to Office (RTO) mandates remotely, or have their own desks, or not be forced to commute in traffic for hours each day, or that there used to be muffins on Mondays. It's no sunshine on the spotless mind scenario here. Our brains just can't do that.

So, instead of severing memories between work and life, we need to consider the whole person coming in to work. What do they need at different life stages, and how can we support those unique needs more effectively?

The whole person

Welcoming the whole person to work is more than recognizing the individual; it's understanding how our personal and professional lives constantly flow together. As I mentioned, we don't just flip a switch and turn one part of brain off and then turn on the other. We carry pieces of our personal lives into work and take parts of our work back home with us.

I know that, for many of us, if we've been up all night with a sick child we're bringing that exhaustion into the office. I've been there – irritability, distractibility and even just struggling to stay awake took a major toll on my ability to perform. Sleep deprivation is no joke. Research finds that across five OECD countries, up to $680 billion in economic output is lost every year due to insufficient sleep.[8]

And it's not just parents. Caregivers, for example, are facing growing demands as more people support ageing parents. Today, about 23 per cent of adults in the US are sandwiched between caring for young children and their ageing parents.[9] That number is 21 per cent in both the UK and Canada.[10] People in their 40s are most likely to be in this position,[11] so with 50 per cent of the world's managers in this age range[12] we want to ensure that they are being properly supported through this phase. Especially since managers have such an impact on the engagement of their direct reports.

It's also about recognizing that each phase of life comes with its own challenges and priorities. Younger employees often crave mentorship, development and maybe a little support with those student loans as they get on their feet. Meanwhile, mid-career folks, especially parents, need flexibility – sometimes it's a later start to drop kids at school or a longer lunch to meet with a caregiver for an ageing parent.

For women in the workplace, menopause can hit right in the middle of a career, just when they're at their peak professionally. Did you know that in 2024, 84 per cent of women surveyed said they want more workplace support for menopause? And yet only 23 per cent of companies offer specific benefits for this life stage.[13] I've heard countless stories of women powering through symptoms like hot flushes and sleeplessness, hoping it doesn't affect their performance.

So why not meet these needs head-on? Organizations like Moody's and Crawford & Company are doing just that. They're providing cooling rooms, flexible schedules, and dedicated menopause benefits. Imagine what it would feel like to work somewhere that truly gets the challenges of each life stage.

To build a workplace that's ready to embrace the whole person, we need to think beyond standard benefits. Let's offer health coverage that meets real needs – fertility support for those starting families or menopause care for women who are feeling the impact. Let's tailor financial planning so it fits whether you're paying off student loans, saving for a home or preparing for retirement. And let's not forget family-friendly policies that cover everything from parental leave to eldercare support.

When we start looking at benefits this way, we're not just supporting employees; we're building a workplace that people want to stay in and grow with. For leaders this means accepting that life and all of its stressful moments will happen, whether we like it or not. So, instead of ignoring these truths, we must embrace them.

Building a flexible culture

A decade ago, I wrote the following: 'Thanks to smartphones, laptops, Wi-Fi and a host of other technologies, we can work in so many other places than a traditional office. Around 2.8 million people in the United Kingdom alone work from home, equalling 10 per cent of total employment.'

Flash forward to 2025 and everything and nothing has changed. People still want to work remotely and stigma still remains. A recent Gallup poll found that 27 per cent want to be fully remote, 53 per cent want to be hybrid and 21 per cent want to be in the office full time.[14]

I quoted a Microsoft whitepaper from 2011 titled 'Work without walls', which was a study by Microsoft, proudly displayed on their website, that claimed that 'the ability to work from outside the office is no longer an employee perk; it is a business imperative'. The study surveyed more than 4,000 information workers in the manufacturing, financial services, retail/hospitality and professional services industries. Among its findings:

- 77 per cent of information workers in financial services would rather work remotely, indicating that a better work/life balance was their number-one reason for preferring to work from home.
- Fewer than 6 in 10 information workers (58 per cent) in manufacturing say their companies have a formal policy of allowing employees to work remotely. Yet 79 per cent of those surveyed stated a preference for working remotely.[15]

So, what would you guess is the reason this remote work practice wasn't widely adopted then? Unfortunately, it feels way too familiar today.

The same Microsoft report found that 'Business leaders assume employees who work remotely and take advantage of the policy are not really working. This is because of the loss of control. Employers lose direct oversight and cannot witness productivity firsthand'.

At the time I called out for change – that this is a major issue and one that we as leaders can easily solve. I wrote:

> Frankly, it should be on us to set specific and measurable goals then track those goals to outcomes. This way, our employees can work at their desks, at home, or at a coffee shop – basically they could work anywhere.

> The way I see it, my time is much more valuable to me than if I were to spend it standing over the shoulders of my staff to ensure they're working. And, by manufacturing this need for our employees to be in a place within certain set hours, then we are simply demanding presence, not productivity. We need to be responsible for establishing frequent, various and meaningful methods of communication, regardless of where our people physically sit.

In 2020, we were forced to test this theory. What the workforce proved is that working remotely can work. And people were actually flourishing.

Despite the data, some CEOs are calling people back to the office. Since we'd made such a full swing during the pandemic it made sense to meet in the middle. This is where hybrid working was born. Some time in the office. Some time working remotely. The number of days and ways to make a hybrid model work varied across organizations – but it worked. And so it remains the most popular working style for the majority of organizations.

As of 2023, approximately 65 per cent of global workplaces had adopted a hybrid work model, reflecting a significant increase from 50 per cent in 2020. This trend indicates a growing acceptance of flexible work arrangements worldwide. In the United States, the adoption of hybrid work is even more pronounced. In the first quarter of 2024, an estimated 54 per cent of office workers were on a hybrid schedule, marking the highest level ever recorded.[16]

These statistics highlight a global shift towards hybrid work environments, with a notable uptick in adoption rates over recent years. No one understood the rationale. All the data showed that hybrid working styles were going well. It was a fair compromise and that flexibility was increasing well-being, work/life harmony and happiness.

In *Why Are We Here?* I write about the power of freedom – how we hold on to our freedom even at great personal risk. This makes people resistant to complying with policies that they perceive are thwarting our freedom.

The reality is, the office experience has always been problematic. A study analyzing data from 17,985 adult commuters between 1991 to 2008 found that increased commuting time was associated with declines in mental health, particularly among individuals with low job control.

Here's a large swathe of the workforce eating something delicious and healthy and then suddenly that was replaced with cold, mushy carrots that have zero nutritional value.

Leaders mandating people back to the office have to acknowledge that it hasn't been going smoothly. It's not just perception either, the data is definitive – RTO mandates don't work.

Nicholas Bloom, Professor of Economics at Stanford, and his team of researchers did a split A/B test where they randomly assigned employees to a three-day or five-day in-office schedule. They partnered with Trip.com, one of the world's largest online travel companies, with 40,000 employees, to test their theory.[17]

The control group went into the office five days a week for six months. The treatment group, went to the office only on Mondays, Tuesdays and Thursdays within the same timeframe.

The research team analysed data from the six-month experiment and subsequent performance reviews for the next two years, and found the two groups showed no difference in performance review grade or promotion, and there was a 1 per cent increase in productivity for the hybrid group.

However, for those working under the hybrid model there was a significantly higher satisfaction rate and a whopping 35 per cent lower attrition. According to their article, 'Quit-rate reductions were largest for female employees. Non-managers and those with the long commutes greater than 1.5 hours also had significantly reduced quit rates under hybrid'.

They also factored in data by the Society of Human Resource Management – each quit costs companies at least 50 per cent of the employees' annual salary, which for Trip.com would mean $30,000 for each quit. In Trip.com's experiment, employees liked hybrid so much that their quit rates fell by more than a third – and saved the company millions of dollars a year.

One of the interesting data points to come out of this experiment was that hybrid employees were working about 1.5 hours less per home day, superficially suggesting these employees were working less. But in examining the data closely, they found hybrid employees put in longer hours on their office days and weekends to make up. Employees shared that they found home-days useful for important activities like a doctor's appointment, taking their children to school or trips, or leisure activities like golf. Because these workers were well motivated by rigorous performance evaluations, they made up for this with longer hours on office days and weekends.

If we want healthy, happy, high-performing workplaces we must look to the data for the answers. But more importantly, action what you learn. And, in this instance, if all the data points to hybrid and flexible working models as the best for our business, then ego shouldn't trump following the facts.

Happiness and the whole person in hard times

When we're integrating our values, emotions and full range of life experiences into our daily experience of work, it boosts engagement and creates a friendlier workplace. But during times of chronic stress, uncertainty and burnout, this approach becomes even more vital.

For many high-performing individuals, especially those with perfectionist tendencies and multiple roles, embracing the whole person is more than a perk – it's a necessity to sustain both well-being and performance.

A key benefit to this strategy is that when we bring our whole selves to work, we reduce cognitive dissonance – the mental conflict we experience when our values or needs clash with our actions. For someone who's driven, perfectionistic and constantly balancing high expectations (this resonates), there can be a significant tension between personal aspirations and professional responsibilities. When we suppress or compartmentalize these parts of ourselves, the dissonance creates a low-level, chronic stress that eats away at our resilience over time.

I feel like we can all relate to juggling a packed schedule, managing teams, or launching a business, all while showing up for our families in a meaningful way and maintaining personal standards of excellence. Without an environment that values and understands this complexity, the internal strain becomes enormous.

This stress can amplify in people with a hard time saying 'no', where pushing personal needs aside becomes a default. Over time, it leads to a persistent feeling of being stretched too thin – causing irritability, decreased focus and even guilt, as we struggle to meet every demand. This is often referred to as cognitive load.

Cognitive load refers to the mental effort required for tasks, and today's workforce is experiencing unprecedented levels of it. In fact, according to research from the American Psychological Association, cognitive overload can impair decision-making, increase anxiety and ultimately lead to burnout. The combination of cognitive load with personal stressors – like family responsibilities – results in a constant background hum of mental strain.[18]

We can reduce the intensity of that persistent noise by working on our psychological flexibility, a concept well-researched in behavioural science, which refers to our ability to adapt to changing circumstances while maintaining our core values.

Scientists describe psychological flexibility as the capacity to be in contact with the present moment, fully aware of one's thoughts, emotions and sensations, and accepting all of them, including the distressing ones.[19] The whole person approach promotes psychological flexibility by encouraging people to be authentic, to show vulnerability and to adjust their expectations in real time. For high achievers with perfectionist tendencies, psychological flexibility can be a lifeline. It allows us to recognize when we're pushing too hard or need to let go, without feeling that we're compromising our values or standards.

In a rapidly changing world filled with unpredictable demands, being psychologically flexible isn't just helpful – it's essential. Particularly in the case of high-performing women, this means understanding that success doesn't mean perfection and that, sometimes, the smartest choice is to prioritize well-being over relentless output. Practising flexibility might mean reassessing priorities, stepping back from nonessential commitments, or simply acknowledging that perfection is not always attainable.

For those of us who are high achievers, psychological safety can help mitigate the fear of falling short. It becomes OK to express the need for a break or to ask for help – both of which are crucial to long-term health and happiness. Without this safety net, perfectionists, in particular, can end up sacrificing their well-being for a standard of performance that's neither sustainable nor fulfilling in the long run.

Happiness at work is often described as a by-product of engagement and purpose, but it's also about experiencing true belonging and acceptance. When we're able to bring our whole selves to work, we experience less tension between 'work self' and 'home self'. This alignment reduces the cognitive dissonance that often arises from managing multiple roles with opposing demands. It also promotes a feeling of authenticity, which is linked to higher levels of well-being and life satisfaction.

The days when I can openly integrate my values and needs into my work are when I feel the most energized and committed. When our workplaces make room for our whole selves, we don't just perform better; we lead happier, more fulfilling lives. Embracing this approach is not just a response to current challenges – it's a way to create work environments that are resilient, adaptable and truly supportive of workplace well-being.

HAPPINESS IN ACTION

Grab your notebook and answer the following questions:

1. Define work/life harmony in your own words.
2. Now look at your definition.
3. Is this definition your current reality?
4. If no, would you be happier if your definition were closer to your reality?
5. If yes, spend the next five days writing down new ways to get to the perfect state of work/life harmony then begin to tackle those goals one by one.
6. If you are already in work/life harmony write down how you are going to maintain this state.

Debunking flexibility myths

- Gather your team for a one-hour discussion.
- Get them to list what flexibility means to them. You'll hear common responses like 'remote work' or 'working from home'. This is how we can reframe that flexibility isn't all about 'where' but instead can also encompass varied work hours, project timelines and task autonomy.
- Discuss 'flexibility dimension' with your team as alternative thinking to 'where' we work.
- Time flexibility: Discuss allowing employees to choose their work hours or adjusting schedules based on productivity peaks.
- Method flexibility: Highlight how employees can be given freedom in approaches, workflows, or tools used to complete tasks.
- Pace flexibility: Allow for pacing adjustments so employees can prioritize mental breaks and manage peak stress times.
- Now commit to experimentation.
- Pilot one new flexibility approach in the coming month and gather feedback.
- Set specific, measurable goals.
- Discuss what worked, share feedback, and iterate on flexible policies.

HAPPY LEARNING!

Read

- Buettner, D (2010) *The Blue Zones: Lessons for living longer from the people who've lived the longest*, National Geographic
- Hsei, T (2010) *Delivering Happiness: A path to profits, passion, and purpose*, Business Plus

Notes

1 Gettysburg College. One third of your life is spent at work, *Gettysburg College*, 2023. www.gettysburg.edu/news/stories?id=79db7b34-630c-4f49-ad32-4ab9ea48e72b (archived at https://perma.cc/QWN9-BERW)
2 Gallup. *State of the Global Workplace 2024 Report*, Gallup, 2024
3 Mercer. 2024 global talent trends, Mercer, 2024. www.mercer.com/insights/people-strategy/future-of-work/global-talent-trends (archived at https://perma.cc/MW2E-CU5T)
4 R Waldinger and M Schulz (2023) *The Good Life: Lessons from the world's longest scientific study of happiness*, Simon & Schuster.
5 R Waldinger and M Schulz (2023) *The Good Life: Lessons from the world's longest scientific study of happiness*, Simon & Schuster.
6 R Chandran. The importance of work-life-balance, Academia, nd. www.academia.edu/7373612/The_Importance_of_Work_Life_Balance (archived at https://perma.cc/HE7M-QDDM)
7 A Perschel. Work-life flow: How Individuals, Zappos, and other innovative companies achieve high engagement, *Global Business and Organizational Excellence*, 2010, 29 (4), 17–30.
8 M Hafner et al. Why sleep matters – The economic costs of insufficient sleep: A cross-country comparative analysis, *RAND Health Quarterly*, 2017, 6 (4). www.rand.org/pubs/periodicals/health-quarterly/issues/v6/n4/11.html (archived at https://perma.cc/NWT2-4MG3)
9 Pew Research Center. More than half of Americans in their 40s are 'sandwiched' between an aging parent and their own children, Pew Research Center, 2022. www.pewresearch.org/short-reads/2022/04/08/more-than-half-of-americans-in-their-40s-are-sandwiched-between-an-aging-parent-and-their-own-children (archived at https://perma.cc/S27E-R436)

10 C Williams. The sandwich generation, Statistics Canada, 2005. www150.statcan.gc.ca/n1/pub/11-008-x/2005001/article/7033-eng.pdf (archived at https://perma.cc/3323-BYL9); Office for National Statistics. Sandwich Generation, GOV.UK, 2019. www.gov.uk/government/statistics/sandwich-generation (archived at https://perma.cc/337P-6VNF)

11 Pew Research Center. More than half of Americans in their 40s are 'sandwiched' between an aging parent and their own children, Pew Research Center, 2022. www.pewresearch.org/short-reads/2022/04/08/more-than-half-of-americans-in-their-40s-are-sandwiched-between-an-aging-parent-and-their-own-children (archived at https://perma.cc/S27E-R436)

12 R Kovach. Meet your new boss: Gen X, *Psychology Today*, 2023. www.psychologytoday.com/us/blog/the-psychology-of-work/202307/meet-your-new-boss-gen-x (archived at https://perma.cc/BR5G-LFMJ)

13 Catalyst. Women call for more menopause support in the workplace in new global survey, Catalyst, 2024. www.catalyst.org/media-release/menopause-workplace-support-global

14 Gallup. Hybrid work, 2024. www.gallup.com/401384/indicator-hybrid-work.aspx (archived at https://perma.cc/EC4M-YUV2)

15 Microsoft. Work without walls: US telework trends 2011, Microsoft, 2011. news.microsoft.com/download/features/2011/05-18Remote.pptx (archived at https://perma.cc/TT7A-TFJ4)

16 FlexOS. Hybrid work statistics and trends, FlexOS, 2023. www.flexos.work/learn/hybrid-work-statistics-and-trends (archived at https://perma.cc/MNC3-ZR78)

17 N Bloom, R Han and J Liang. Hybrid working from home improves retention without damaging performance, *Nature*, 2024, 630, 920–25. doi.org/10.1038/s41586-024-07500-2 (archived at https://perma.cc/PA4R-ETV6)

18 American Psychological Association. Burnout and stress are everywhere, *Monitor on Psychology*, 2022. www.apa.org/monitor/2022/01/special-burnout-stress (archived at https://perma.cc/G5C4-S3LM)

19 Science Direct. Psychological flexibility, Science Direct, 2021. www.sciencedirect.com/topics/psychology/psychological-flexibility (archived at https://perma.cc/J5XK-Z8HK)

7

A happier approach to change

Change is hard

Change is one of the most common causes of stress inside organizations. Leaders struggle to inspire their teams amongst constantly shifting priorities, while individual employees feel uncertain about the future and lack the insights to calm their fears.

There are many reasons that change occurs in an organization, but it may feel like the amount of change we experience at work is overwhelming. Especially since 2020 when the world started spinning out of control. With globalization and constant innovation of technology, we're facing a rapidly evolving business environment.

Digital and social media and mobile adaptability have revolutionized business, and the effect of this is an ever-growing need for change, and subsequent change management.

The development of new technology also has a secondary effect of increasing the accessibility and therefore responsibility of knowledge. Organizational change is largely motivated by competition and that requires immediately adaptability or the potential to be left behind.

With the business environment undergoing so much change, the ability to manage and adapt through it is a necessary capacity required in the workplace today. Yet, as we are all very much aware, major and rapid organizational change is intensely difficult.

Why?

Because the deeply imbedded infrastructure, culture, and patterns of organizations often reflect a stubborn 'imprint' of past periods, which are resistant to major change.

In their seminal 2013 paper 'Imprinting: Toward a multilevel theory', Cambridge University Professor Christopher Marquis and Professor at the

University of Toronto's Rotman School of Management András Tilcsik explored how organizations are influenced by their founding environments, a concept known as imprinting.[1]

They argue that elements from an organization's inception can persist over time, affecting its adaptability to change. This persistence can pose challenges for change management, as ingrained practices and cultures may resist new initiatives. Understanding these deep-seated influences is crucial for effectively implementing organizational change.

If you ask employees how they're feeling about work lately, chances are you'll hear some recurring words: stressed, anxious, uncertain. And it's not hard to see why. Change fatigue is a very real phenomena because constant pivoting and responding to new disruptions has become normalized as the new way of doing business.

It's also showing no signs of slowing down.

As companies race to keep up with rapid technological advancements, shifting work models, economic uncertainty and constant restructuring, it's time to ask an important question: are we pushing our people beyond what's sustainable?

Let's analyse what's driving this stress, and what organizations – and leaders – can do to help.

The big disruptors

In 1789 Benjamin Franklin famously wrote to French physicist Jean-Baptiste Le Roy, 'Our new Constitution is now established, and has an appearance that promises permanency; but in this world nothing can be said to be certain, except death and taxes'.[2]

I would argue that if Benjamin Franklin were alive and well today, he would have adjusted this statement to include that nothing can be said to be certain, except death and taxes *and* uncertainty. Especially when it comes to leading in today's world of work where we are in a chronic state of rapid and persistent shift. Here's why:

Rapid technological advancements

The swift integration of AI and automation is reshaping job roles and workflows. The World Economic Forum's 'Future of jobs 2023' indicates that by 2027 businesses anticipate that 44 per cent of workers' core skills will be disrupted, with AI being a major contributor. This rapid evolution requires employees to continually adapt, leading to increased stress and uncertainty.[3]

This projection illustrates that nearly half of today's skillsets may be inadequate in just a few years, pushing employees to acquire new competencies at a faster pace than ever before. For some, this transition to AI-augmented work is exciting, offering opportunities for innovation and efficiency. However, for others, the pressure to adapt and reskill can be overwhelming, especially as the need for constant learning clashes with daily workload demands.

In my latest LinkedIn Learning course, Balancing AI Adoption with Workforce Optimization, I discuss how employees are often left to balance their current responsibilities with the pressure to stay current in a rapidly evolving field, which can lead to increased stress and burnout.

As AI transforms workflows, digital literacy has become a critical skill across roles that previously did not require advanced technological know-how. Many workers now need to develop at least a foundational understanding of AI concepts, data analysis and digital tools to remain competitive. This shift is especially challenging for mid-career professionals who may not have been trained in these areas but are now expected to adapt quickly.

Here is where emotional intelligence is enormously valuable. Adaptability, has become a non-negotiable requirement in the age of AI. Employers are increasingly seeking individuals who can not only perform their jobs but also anticipate and embrace continuous change. While this can drive innovation, the demand for constant adaptability can create cognitive strain as workers are required to frequently re-learn and adjust to new tools, processes, and expectations. Over time, this need for flexibility without sufficient support or training can lead to anxiety, self-doubt, and stress.

One of the most significant stressors related to AI integration is uncertainty around job security. While AI has the potential to create new job categories, it also displaces certain roles, particularly those with repetitive tasks that can be easily automated.

When I'm speaking directly to CEOs or with audiences globally, I often mention how and why the pace of change is putting strain on employees, how the pace of change can strain employees, particularly when organizations implement new technologies without adequate support or training. Employees need clear pathways to reskill or upskill, along with structured resources to help them adapt without feeling overwhelmed. Leading companies are beginning to prioritize 'digital empathy', recognizing that implementing AI requires a balance between innovation and human support.

However, not all companies are proactive in these efforts, and many employees are left to navigate these changes alone. To mitigate stress and uncertainty, organizations must actively communicate the purpose behind AI adoption, provide learning opportunities, and foster a culture that encourages adaptability without penalizing employees for needing time to learn. Creating a supportive environment where employees feel equipped to face these changes can reduce anxiety, improve job satisfaction and build resilience within the workforce.

How can we fix it?

One of the ways to reduce this future-focused stress is to implement programming that tackles anxiety and chronic stress in general. Cognitive behavioural interventions (CBI) focus on identifying and changing negative thought patterns that contribute to anxiety. These can be used to help employees reframe their thoughts about AI, moving from fear to a more positive and constructive outlook.

Managers can be trained in CBI, which helps them to recognize signs of negative thinking patterns in their teams, such as employees expressing fear about AI taking over their jobs or feeling overwhelmed by new technology. At an organizational level, companies can provide access to CBI resources, such as online modules or coaching sessions, that help employees develop resilience against AI-related stress. When these interventions are incorporated into the broader employee well-being strategy we foster a more psychologically safe workplace.

Psychologically safe workplaces benefit from environments in which we can speak up, ask questions or express concerns without fear of negative consequences. This can be done at the manager level through regular team meetings where open dialogue is encouraged, while organization-wide initiatives like anonymous feedback channels, regular town hall meetings and leadership training focused on empathy and active listening builds trust and reduces anxiety overall.

We also want to provide access to mental health professionals and programming that is focused on reducing workplace stress. A happier, healthier workforce is a higher-performing one. If you want to get people excited and ready for change, they can't be chronically stressed and burned out.

We also have to keep vigilant by looking out for signs that AI anxiety is still present. They look like:

- Increased absenteeism or turnover which may indicate that employees are experiencing high levels of stress or dissatisfaction related to AI.

Investigate further by conducting exit interviews or stay interviews where we investigate job satisfaction before our employee leaves. We can also lean on focus groups to understand if AI-related anxiety is a contributing factor.

- A drop in engagement levels like less participation in meetings, lower productivity, a lack of enthusiasm or more emotional volatility, can signal that employees are struggling. One-on-one conversations, pulse surveys and offering to provide additional support is helpful here.
- If employees continue to avoid using AI tools, this can be a big tell. It tends to suggest that there is underlying anxiety or a lack of confidence in their abilities. If that's the case, provide targeted training and support. Bring your employee into the decision-making process so you both can decide what training is needed.

When we approach AI anxiety from a behavioural and psychological perspective, we tackle the issue way further upstream. This makes it easier to motivate individuals and teams to adopt and optimize AI technology later on.

Shifts in work models

The transition to hybrid and remote work models has introduced complexities in communication, collaboration, and work/life balance. The World Economic Forum notes that by 2027 businesses predict that almost half of workers' core skills will be disrupted, necessitating significant adjustments in work structures.[4]

This shift to more remote work has led to increased mistrust, which is significantly impacting employee happiness. Employee monitoring has radically increased.

We witnessed the firing of remote and hybrid workers for using mouse jiggler devices to simulate active computer use, highlighting a growing trend among employees to evade constant management scrutiny.

The real issue is that employees feel the need to use tools like these in the first place. They should be able to take minor breaks without penalty and this just reflects the pressures of always-on work cultures.

Other experts agree. They suggest that this practice reveals deeper issues within workplace environments that demand continuous activity and close monitoring, which can be incompatible with varied work paces and lead to employee dissatisfaction.

Employers are urged to focus more on outcomes and productivity metrics rather than monitoring keystrokes and mouse movements. Current disengagement and low enthusiasm among workers, exacerbated by rigid post-pandemic return-to-office policies, indicate an urgent need to reassess management practices and work expectations.

Tracking employees is nothing new, especially in industries like logistics or customer service where efficiency is tied directly to movement. However, the idea of expanding this practice to a broader set of knowledge workers raises significant concerns about employee privacy, autonomy and morale.

A new study finds that the use of electronic monitoring in the workplace can create 'communication privacy turbulence' which arises when organizational culture prioritizes control over freedom. This can lead to negative psychological effects on employees, including a significant erosion of trust.[5]

The American Psychological Association (APA) highlights that employees subjected to electronic surveillance often report higher levels of stress and anxiety. The APA's data shows that about 32 per cent of employees who are monitored report poor mental health compared to those who are not monitored.[6]

Tracking employees may seem like a practical solution, but it neglects to understand the deeper psychological needs baked into human behaviour. And it feels creepy. We hired adults to work for us. Let's treat them like adults.

When you demonstrate a lack of trust – whether by limiting remote work or by tracking employees – you're not just affecting the logistics of where work happens; you're impacting well-being, creativity, and long-term loyalty. Instead, companies should be thinking about how to build environments that people *want* to return to.

So, if tracking isn't the answer, what is?

Leaders need look no further than the concept of job crafting – which allows employees to redesign their roles, responsibilities and even the way they view their work to better fit their interests and skills. The concept was pioneered by psychologists Amy Wrzesniewski and Jane Dutton in the early 2000s, and it has since become a central strategy in positive psychology and organizational well-being. Job crafting is rooted in the idea that when employees actively shape their roles, they experience a greater sense of control and meaning in their work, which can buffer against stress and burnout.

The practice of job crafting typically involves three main strategies:

1. **Task crafting:** Altering the types of tasks you engage in, such as taking on more projects that play to your strengths or allow for creativity, and reducing tasks that feel draining or monotonous.
2. **Relational crafting:** Changing how, and with whom, you interact at work to build more supportive and meaningful connections. This could mean collaborating with colleagues who inspire you or finding ways to mentor or support others.
3. **Cognitive crafting:** Shifting the way you think about your job, reframing tasks in ways that align with your values or connect to a larger purpose. For instance, a customer service representative might view their role as 'helping people solve problems' rather than simply 'answering questions'.

I've seen first-hand how job crafting can transform the way we feel about our work. Research has shown that job crafting has measurable benefits on our well-being and resilience. In a longitudinal study from 2017, researchers found that employees who engaged in job crafting reported higher levels of job satisfaction, lower stress and increased motivation over time. Following participants over a year, the study revealed that those who actively shaped their roles developed a greater sense of purpose and fulfilment.[7]

One reason job crafting is so effective is that it taps into our intrinsic motivation – the kind that comes from doing what we genuinely enjoy, not just for a salary. When we engage in tasks that align with our interests and values, we feel a deeper connection to our work. This approach is especially powerful in today's hybrid or remote work settings, where we often have to create structure and meaning for ourselves.

In our current work environment, where rapid changes and evolving expectations are the norm, job crafting offers a proactive way to manage change and build resilience. Encouraging employees to craft their roles doesn't just benefit them – it benefits everyone – by creating a workplace where people feel more in control and aligned with their personal values. For instance, an employee adapting to hybrid work might shape their tasks to focus on project-based work that can be done remotely, while also making time for regular virtual catch-ups with team members to maintain connection and support.

From a psychological perspective, job crafting supports three core needs defined by Self-Determination Theory (SDT) developed by Edward Deci and Richard Ryan: autonomy, competence and relatedness.

- Autonomy is the need to have control over one's actions – when we feel we have a say in how we approach our work, we're naturally more motivated.
- Competence is the need to feel effective in what we do, which is strengthened when we craft our roles to highlight our strengths and passions.
- Relatedness is our need to feel connected to others, and job crafting lets us build those meaningful interactions that make work feel less like a solo endeavour and more like a shared journey.[8]

Job crafting can be a mindset shift that empowers us to shape our work in a way that brings us joy and resilience. Especially as we navigate the complexities of new and migrating work models that are still yet to be fully defined. By fostering this strategy, we're helping people take ownership of their roles, adapt to changes, and cultivate well-being.

Economic uncertainty

When we talk about financial wellness, it's deeply personal. For far too many workers today, it's about the stress that creeps in when trying to balance budgets that don't quite stretch far enough, the sleepless nights spent worrying over bills and the constant adjustments made just to make ends meet. And with rising cost of living and ever-present job insecurity, these financial worries aren't going away anytime soon. So, how can leaders step up to make a real difference?

First, let's think about financial wellness from a psychological perspective. At its core, financial stress isn't just about money; it's about security and control. When we feel financially vulnerable, it's easy for anxiety to take over. As leaders, one of the most powerful things we can do is create a space where employees feel a sense of stability, even when external forces are shaking things up.

This could mean offering financial wellness programmes that go beyond surface-level budgeting tips and get into personalized financial planning resources or workshops on managing debt and saving for the future. When people feel equipped to handle their finances, it's like a weight lifts off their shoulders, giving them more mental space to focus on their work and well-being.

Not everyone has had the chance to build up their financial know-how, and that's OK. Offering bite-sized 'micro-lessons' on financial literacy can help. Short, 10-minute modules that cover basics like budgeting, saving or managing credit can be hugely beneficial. You could make these accessible on demand so employees can explore topics at their own pace, without feeling overwhelmed by a whole programme. By breaking down financial concepts into easy, actionable steps, employees get useful information without feeling judged or overloaded.

Similar to open office hours, companies can offer financial wellness drop-in sessions where employees can meet with financial advisers or planners for no-cost advice. These sessions can cover topics like managing debt, prioritizing bills, or planning for future expenses. Knowing there's a judgement-free, approachable place to ask questions and get advice can make all the difference in relieving financial stress. Plus, it can foster a sense of community around managing these challenges together.

Sometimes, just having someone to talk to makes financial stress feel more manageable. Encouraging peer-support systems – where employees can pair up to support each other in setting small financial goals – can create a culture of mutual support. These aren't formal coaching sessions, just a way to share tips, set small goals and check in periodically. It's low-key but can create a real sense of solidarity and accountability, turning financial wellness into something employees can work on together, rather than facing it alone.

Each of these interventions is designed to feel approachable, empowering and respectful of employees' realities. By introducing simple, specific supports, leaders can show they're not just aware of financial stress but actively creating spaces and systems to help employees manage it, both practically and mentally.

Another big piece of this puzzle is creating a culture where it's OK to talk about financial stress. We often keep money worries to ourselves, but when we feel safe to speak up it can be incredibly freeing. Leaders can play a key role here by normalizing conversations around financial wellness and even sharing their own stories of navigating economic challenges. When we know we're not alone, it builds community and reduces the isolation that financial stress often brings.

So, where does happiness come into this? Financial stress isn't just about anxiety – it impacts our overall well-being and how we experience joy in our day-to-day lives. When we feel financially secure, we're in a better mental state to focus on the things that make us happy and fulfilled. Leaders who recognize this connection can take meaningful steps to boost happiness at work by offering flexible benefits that adapt to employees' needs, like emergency financial assistance, student loan repayment support or even childcare subsidies. These initiatives tell employees, 'We see you, and we're here to help,' which fosters a sense of belonging and loyalty.

Ultimately, happiness at work isn't about one-off perks or flashy benefits; it's about creating a foundation where people feel supported as whole individuals, financial worries included.

Organizational restructuring

When our workplace goes through big changes like mergers, new technology rollouts or a shift in work models, it can feel like the ground is shifting under us. Over the last few years we've been pivoting like a spinning top. Whether it's adapting to a new role, building new team dynamics or adjusting to AI-driven tasks, these transitions are disrupting our routines and adding far too much stress. But with some intentional strategies leaders can help make these changes feel manageable, even positive, for everyone involved. Here are a few suggestions:

- When everything else is shifting, holding on to small, familiar routines can provide a sense of stability. Leaders can encourage teams to keep certain 'anchor' habits – like a daily check-in, end-of-week wrap-up, or team lunch. These little rituals give us something familiar to lean on, helping employees feel grounded and supported in the midst of change.
- Integrating new technology, like AI, doesn't have to mean overwhelming employees with day-long training sessions. Instead, think about offering short, manageable skill-building 'snack breaks' that cover specific skills in 15–20 minute segments. These mini-sessions are less daunting and give people time to absorb and apply new knowledge without the stress of trying to learn everything all at once.
- With flexible work arrangements on the rise, leaders can make flexibility feel like a win–win. Normalizing flex days that employees can use to balance office and remote work allows for productivity while also respecting personal needs. It also gives employees autonomy when they may be feeling like everything is out of their control.
- Open dialogue goes a long way in reducing change fatigue. Leaders can set the tone by being upfront about the challenges of change, while also

actively listening to employees' concerns. This might mean dedicating time during team meetings for check-ins, or creating anonymous feedback options where employees can share their thoughts. When we're able to speak up without fear of judgement, it boosts our sense of belonging and psychological safety.

- Exhaustion and fatigue is a real risk when we're constantly adapting, so why not create 'recharge corners' where employees can take a quick break? It can just be a quiet room to get space from the mental noise, a cosy nook or even a corner with some comfortable seating and plants can offer employees a brief, calm space to decompress. By encouraging these mini-breaks, we're prioritizing mental well-being and showing that it's OK to pause when needed.
- In times of transition, the process can be just as valuable as the outcome. Leaders can boost morale by recognizing the small wins along the way – whether it's learning a new skill, demonstrating healthy collaboration, solving a problem or simply showing resilience in the face of uncertainty. Acknowledging progress reminds employees that they're doing a great job adapting, even if things still feel in flux.
- Introducing a regular 'Well-being Wednesday' (or any other day that works) can be a great way to keep happiness and well-being front and centre. It could be as simple as taking time to eat lunch together, going for a walk, or reminding your teams about the company's programmes and benefits they can leverage.

These initiatives remind us that work can be a place that genuinely cares for our well-being, creating a culture of support that extends beyond the typical work tasks.

Change can be daunting, but with simple, specific interventions we can help employees feel more secure, valued and happy even amidst uncertainty.

Ignoring change won't make it go away

At one point in our own lives we stopped and looked around, only to realize that we were in a paradigm shift. Like when Blockbuster got Netflixed. Something had suddenly and dramatically shifted the zeitgeist and it would change how we worked and lived.

My moment of awakening happened while I was living in San Jose, California and working in Communications for a global HR firm. It was during the social media boom and it was an exciting and rapidly shifting time to be in my field.

I remember Facebook coming to town, LinkedIn setting up shop and Twitter sending out its first tweet. At the time, chief marketing officers (CMOs) thought it was a fad but were warming up to it. CEOs had no interest at all in making budget for social media. They would say it was because there was no way 'tweeting' would become commonplace. When I asked one CEO of a well-known global brand about his social media strategy, he said with disdain, 'Twitter is just too silly for anyone, never mind executives. Tweeting would only make them look stupid.'

But all of us who were seeing signs that social media wasn't going away knew that this rhetoric around social media's 'silliness' was only a disguise of pure fear. This level of disruption in the way we communicated with and to each other would mean a massive learning curve for senior leaders, who would have no clue where to begin.

Around the same time, I recall attending a workshop at Cinequest, a film festival based in San Jose, where I listened to Steve Wozniak make a scary prediction to a room full of filmmakers. He got on stage and told everyone in the room they would be filming in digital and it could be on a camera so small it would fit into your phone (ironically he was pointing to his Palm Pilot that night). Although he was met with disbelief in the audience it was only a few short years before the entire industry saw Wozniak's predictions come true.

As leaders, we become nervous about change because we start thinking about the sheer size and weight of scaling our efforts and resources. However, if we better understood how to navigate change and therefore minimized the negative impacts from it, we wouldn't get caught off guard. And lack of preparedness can be even more stressful for employees experiencing change fatigue. You only have to go back to mid 2020 to remember how exhausting it was to be in constant reaction mode.

The neuroscience of change

So, why do we react negatively to change? Why does our cultural imprinting have to be so stubborn?

Although transformation is constant and we may think we enjoy change, our lazy brains prefer things to stay the same. Well-formed decision frameworks are cognitively easier so we like to rely on them. Despite how much we enjoy novelty and the many benefits of change – like psychological growth and emotional development – our brains seem to rebel against change.

The brain's first response to change is to generate a state of cognitive dissonance, registering a discomfort between what it expects and what it now needs to do.[9] The typical sequence of events in our brain goes something like this:

1. Activation of the limbic network as the impact of the change is realized.
2. Activation of the pre-frontal cortex to create a rational explanation for the change.
3. Exhaustion of the pre-frontal cortex resources due to managing the emotional reaction, which often leads to poor mental state and loss of productivity and focus.
4. Renewed cognitive activity as new behavioural skills are mastered and rewiring of neuro-pathways takes place.
5. New behaviours become habitual and reside in the basal ganglia.

Now that we have this critical information, we can harness that understanding by handling change management with neuroscience and psychological sciences at the core of our strategies and tactics. One such tactic, critical to moving successfully through these stages, is:

1. Setting goals (to override habitual and emotional reactions).
2. Giving rewards to activate dopamine release and maintain motivation during the rewiring stage.
3. Acknowledging emotional reactions.
4. Helping people gain insight into what the change actually means to individuals.
5. Helping people create a clear picture of their role during the change.
6. Encouraging people to set clear goals for the future.
7. Reinforcing and rewarding behaviour directed towards these goals.
8. Paying attention to how we as leaders may de-escalate a threat response and focus on creating an environment that feels rewarding.

According to Emma Seppälä, Science Director of Stanford University's Center for Compassion and Altruism Research and Education and author of

The Happiness Track, our state of mind is the key to navigating change in a healthy way.[10]

A happier approach to change

In our interview, Emma Seppälä suggested that we can't control our external circumstances, and things change constantly whether at work or in our personal lives. The only thing we can have a say over is the state of our mind. That's why it's so important to cultivate resilience – the ability to generate more inner peace, to stay calm in the face of chaos, to remain emotionally intelligent as we communicate with others despite conflict or hurt feelings, to make good decisions even when we're feeling upset.

After years of consulting Fortune 500 leaders and employees in the areas of positive organizational psychology, health psychology, cultural psychology, well-being and resilience, Emma Seppälä learned proactive ways to mitigate the negative effects of change: build internal resilience, whether that's through meditation or breathing exercises – anything that helps train your nervous system to be more solid and more calm, your thoughts and emotions to be less overwhelming.

Since we are in a time of persistent change, the more tools we have at our disposal the easier it will be to adapt. And that perception of resources is key to calming an anxious mind.

Why well-being at work isn't working

According to BambooHR's 2023 Employee Happiness Index, sadly titled 'The great gloom', 'From the start of 2020 through the present, employee happiness has steadily declined at a rate of 6%. But 2023 has seen a steep and steady drop, with a decrease of 9% in employee net promoter score (eNPS) since January, declining at a rate 10x faster than the previous three years'.

The research team surveyed 60,000 global employees and found that unhappiness was even higher in 2023 than at the peak of the pandemic. The report found that most employees aren't feeling highs and lows but rather they are feeling 'a sense of resignation or even apathy'.[11]

Employee net promoter score, a numeric rating of how likely employees are to recommend their organization as a place to work, has fallen off a cliff since the peak of the pandemic. The report shares an analysis of 1.4 billion eNPS scores since 2020 that show they are declining at a rate ten times faster than in the previous three years.

With the global wellness industry now worth $5.6 trillion[12] and the global corporate wellness market size predicted to grow from $61.27 billion in 2023 to $85.02 billion by 2030,[13] shouldn't we be wondering why our people are so apathetic and resigned?

The answer is simple. We're getting it wrong.

New research by William Fleming, social scientist and Unilever Research Fellow at the Well-being Research Centre at the University of Oxford, rocked the well-being industry and became a viral mainstream media topic. Not only because it was provocative research, but in a bold move, Fleming was poking holes in his existing research and that of his peers.

Published in 2024, Fleming had analysed 46,336 workers in 233 organizations and found that despite 'individual-level well-being interventions, including resilience training, mindfulness and well-being apps... across multiple subjective well-being indicators, participants appear no better off'.[14]

Fleming found that for higher-paying salaried employees, programmes like resilience training actually had a *negative* effect on well-being. Employees most impacted were specifically executive women who were trying to find time for the training while juggling competing schedules. This isn't all that surprising. Wouldn't you feel frustrated that your employer's response to burning you out was to offer you training so you can be more resilient to them burning you out?

This is the definition of tone deaf.

When hygiene is missing, motivation is at a deficit. I will repeat, well-being should not be workload. Well-being shouldn't be workload.

I believe that this is a shocking and yet not surprising discovery. It's actually validating for others like me in this field who've been saying for years that downstream tactics don't work. One of the most compelling aspects of Fleming's research, in my opinion, is the discovery of the one individual-level well-being intervention that did work – altruism. Organizations high in altruistic behaviours, which included tactics like volunteering, showed higher self-reported well-being.

BetterUp is a virtual coaching platform that invests in psychological and wellness research with their Center for Purpose and Performance, headed up by Adam Grant. They describe altruism as 'unselfish behavior intended to benefit others. It involves some kind of goal-directed action that helps improve someone else's welfare'.[15] They suggest that if you're altruistic, 'you're doing things out of kindness and a sincere desire to help – not because you feel obligated. Your motivation stems from a genuine concern for others' well-being, even if that means putting your own aside'.

Let's pause on this. After decades of rigorous analysis, the one well-being initiative that Fleming says works is... drum roll please... kindness. Despite a solution as simple as this, kindness is at risk. And if we as leaders don't stick up for it – preserve it – we'll find ourselves in an even more polarizing world.

The type of leaders that take these kinds of initiatives on, despite their questions and fears, are those who exhibit high levels of openness, self-awareness, critical analysis, bravery and a keen knowledge of their company's character. Unfortunately, it's hard to be a human-centred leader in a world where growth at all costs is still the norm. But we've seen leaders who've exhibited these behaviours in the past, and despite the hardship they're viewed as the most prolific leaders in history. So, who are they?

Leaders taking leaps

When thinking about disruption, we have to be able to step back and imagine leapfrogging our present state, not just iterating on it. No transformation of great scale occurs without innovation, hard work and significant change – or disrupting the norm – and the change we are going through now will be no exception. Henry Ford, founder of the Ford Motor Company, once said that, had he asked people what they really wanted, they would have said 'faster horses'.

The greatest leaders in history took giant leaps. They may not have recognized that they were leading a happiness strategy but, regardless, it would turn out to be a winning strategy. We're missing our great leaders right now – the ones who were willing to sacrifice it all for the good of humankind. Today's CEOs may not be able to cure all the causes of our stress, but they should most definitely care.

Lately, the world feels angrier, more prone to conflict – less happy. I believe that it has a lot to do with our global political environment and how those have been breaking the rules of engagement. At first it was shocking. How can people behave this way? It feels cognitively dissonant – like our brain can't compute what we're seeing. But since we've had to exist in this state for so long our brains have started to normalize the behaviour.

This is not what we want. We need to be reminded of the type of leader we use to look up to. The kind of leader that would inspire prosocial change. The kind of leader that would battle against a bully, not become one. We are all leaders – all of us – and we need to be reminded to step up and try harder – to be better – because it matters today more than ever.

You might think you know everything about the following leaders, but I hope to offer a fresh perspective on their courage and vision. My goal is to inspire us to reach back in time, drawing from these timeless traits to shape our own future leadership strategies.

Nelson Mandela

After 27 years incarcerated for fighting against apartheid, Nelson Mandela went on to become South Africa's first black president. While in prison he had to tolerate living conditions that consisted of a damp concrete cell measuring 8 × 7 feet with a straw mat on which to sleep. Other prisoners harassed him until he was reassigned to work in a lime quarry. What should have been a relief from the harassment wound up being another setback, as the glare from the lime permanently damaged his eyesight.[16]

At night, Mandela worked on his law degree, but newspapers were forbidden so he would often find himself in solitary confinement for possessing smuggled news clippings. Finally, in 1980, after many years of turmoil and exhausting effort, Mandela earned his degree in law. It wasn't until his release in 1990 and his subsequent win in the presidential elections four years later that he got a chance to use it.

What is most demonstrative of Mandela's grace came just after he was released from imprisonment. Although he could have been jaded, angry and vengeful, he was the opposite. Mandela went out of his way to invite his former jailers for tea and then to his presidential inauguration. He welcomed them with genuine warmth, despite the hardships they had overseen. When asked why he did this, Mandela explained that harbouring resentment would only keep him emotionally imprisoned. 'We must be generous,' he would say.

This act showed incredible humility and the belief that understanding others, even those who may have wronged you, is essential to true leadership.

He also consistently met people where they were at. Whether you lived in a homeless camp or were a political dignitary, everyone was equal.

Nelson Mandela's interactions with Betsie Verwoerd in 1995, the widow of Hendrik Verwoerd, one of the chief architects of apartheid, was another striking example of his tolerance, empathy and deep commitment to reconciliation.[17] Mandela's visit was not about demanding apologies or asking her to reflect on her husband's role in apartheid. Instead, he listened to her, respected her and sought to understand her perspective. Mandela knew the importance of tolerance and sought to model what he called a 'rainbow nation' – one in which former adversaries could find common ground.

These examples aren't just one-offs – this was who Mandela was at the core.

During the Rugby World Cup, also in 1995, Mandela donned the jersey of South African rugby captain Francois Pienaar – a white man who symbolized the sport long dominated by apartheid symbolism. Rugby had been a point of division between Black and white South Africans, but Mandela understood its unifying potential. By wearing Pienaar's number six jersey, Mandela demonstrated that humility and tolerance could bridge divides.[18]

And when Mandela became President, many expected him to use his position to seek revenge on the apartheid leaders. Instead, he treated them with respect, even extending forgiveness to his predecessor, F W de Klerk. De Klerk was invited to serve as Mandela's deputy in the new government, a powerful symbol of humility and a reminder that Mandela prioritized unity over personal grievances.

These stories highlight Mandela's unshakable humility and commitment to tolerance, which is a stark contrast to some of the ego-driven leadership we are seeing more frequently today. What can this teach us?

As humans, this reminds us that we have the capacity to overcome almost anything. Regardless of how enduring the sacrifice, we are built with coping skills and the resilience needed not just to survive, but to thrive.

As leaders, this teaches us how to put aside our ego and do what is best for the greater good of the organization. It forces us to decide whether we want to be angry in the moment, or be forgiving. We need to constantly ask ourselves: is there an opportunity here to tie people together, and how can I represent that in my language, in my communication and in my leadership? What signal can I give to those who are looking to me for guidance that I am here with grace, dignity and respect for their happiness and well-being?

It doesn't need to be grand gestures; it just needs to be consistent. How can we visualize the story of Mandela drinking tea with Betsie Verwoerd to our advantage? Is there a way to turn threats into opportunities? Enemies into friends? Mistrust into believing again?

Modelling this type of leadership is what we *all* need right now – leaders with the type of tolerance, humility and forward-looking hopefulness that brings us together instead of driving us apart. It's up to us to show others that this is still possible, even in divisive times.

Jimmy Carter

Jimmy Carter's life and leadership are filled with stories of humility, empathy and tolerance that set him apart from other leaders then and now.

Some would argue that he made some terrible missteps in his Presidency – and actually Carter would be the first to agree. This is what sets him apart from today's leaders – his sense of accountability. As Alexander Pope so famously stated, 'To err is human; to forgive, divine.' This is how Carter lived out his leadership.

During the Iran hostage crisis in 1979, Carter faced relentless criticism. He took full responsibility, never blaming others or seeking to dodge criticism, even when it hurt his re-election campaign. This willingness to take accountability – a quality rare in politics – revealed a true humility and sense of duty to those he served. When the hostages were finally freed, Carter met them personally and apologized for his role and for what they had endured.[19]

Carter always maintained relationships with those who sharply criticized him, demonstrating tolerance and forgiveness even when it wasn't politically expedient. He worked with Ronald Reagan on issues like nuclear disarmament and election monitoring, despite their political differences. Carter believed that even former adversaries had something to contribute, exemplifying his belief that bridges can be built in even the most polarized environments.

He was an advocate for global peace, which was illustrated during the 1978 Camp David Accords. Despite the cultural and historical animosity between Egypt and Israel, Carter's patience and willingness to serve as a mediator eventually led to a treaty.

After leaving office, Carter didn't retreat into a life of privilege or lucrative speaking opportunities. Instead, he spent decades building homes for the underserved through Habitat for Humanity. Even in his nineties, Carter would show up on construction sites, hammer in hand, often working alongside volunteers in extreme heat or cold. His willingness to physically labour for others, regardless of his former status, exemplifies a selfless, servant-hearted humility.

In 2015, after being diagnosed with advanced melanoma, Carter was offered specialized and aggressive treatment. Instead of rushing to seek the best available resources, Carter asked that the treatment be made available to all his fellow patients at Emory University Hospital, regardless of their status or insurance. This act underscored Carter's belief that no life is worth more than another, a profoundly humble viewpoint that is rare among those who have achieved his level of influence.[20]

In an age when many leaders seek personal gain and recognition, Carter's example reminds us of what it looks like to lead with empathy and an unwavering dedication to the well-being of others.

We are also in an era with zero tolerance for mistakes – 'cancel culture' gone overboard – and we need to find our way back to a more forgiving world. Egregious behaviour shouldn't be tolerated and standing up to bullies is crucial. But remember, to forgive is divine.

Since change is so hard, we had better make those changes count. I believe that investing in caring companies is the future. We want our employers to care about us and to care about the world. So, let's discuss how to get there by looking at those companies that are killing it with kindness.

Below are recommended reading and some activities to get started on.

HAPPINESS IN ACTION

Embrace a new routine

Learn to love a new way of behaving:

- Do you wear a watch every day? Switch wrists for an entire week and see how it feels.
- Is your morning routine set in stone? Change it up. Eat first and get dressed after, or vice versa. Just take a week and do it differently.
- Do you have a ritual at work? Instead of eating at your desk during lunch or having coffee at exactly 9.15 every day on the nose, go for a walk or drink tea instead.

Whatever the change is, just make sure you notice it. Write down how it felt to forget that your watch is on the other wrist or how badly you wanted to wash your hair before eating toast. Before you go to bed at night, write a note about those small inconveniences. Then take it one step further and imagine yourself in the shoes of an employee who was just transferred to another office location, or someone who was just promoted. We all assume change like promotions or new opportunities to advance are terrific, and for many they are. However, change is still challenging. So, spend some time working on empathy-building as it relates to supporting your people through change – particularly if you're just about to tell them about a new happiness strategy you're going to implement. You'll most definitely want to make sure they're ready for that level of shift, perhaps encouraging them to put the watch back where it belongs.

Rediscover the joy of work through job crafting

- Have employees identify their strengths, values and interests, then outline how they could make small adjustments to their tasks, relationships or mindset to align their jobs more closely with their goals.
- Engage in bi-weekly reflection exercises where employees spend a few minutes at the end of each week reflecting on which tasks energized them and which drained them. This process can help them understand areas for potential crafting and proactively seek tasks or collaborations that increase motivation.
- Collaborative job design sessions pull together teams who are encouraged to brainstorm ways they can collectively craft their tasks and roles to better align with individual strengths. This fosters a sense of shared ownership over the team's work and helps team members better understand each other's roles.

How do I want to change so others will too?

Back to Q&A time. This will help to get your mind contemplating how you want to be the change to inspire it in others.

Write down a major change that could or should occur in your life:

- How do think about this change?
- What are the good things that might come from this change?
- What do you fear about this change?
- How will this change affect others in your life?
- Who would support you in this change and how?
- What are the resources available to you?
- What do you think would be an appropriate timetable for this change?

HAPPY LEARNING!

Read

- Senge, P (1999) *The Fifth Discipline: The art and practice of the learning organization*, Random House
- Senge, P (1999) *The Dance of Change: The challenges of sustaining momentum in learning organizations*, Nicholas Brealey Publishing
- Seppälä, E (2016) *The Happiness Track*, HarperOne

Notes

1 C Marquis and A Tilcsik. Imprinting: Toward a multilevel theory, *Academy of Management Annals*, 2013, 7 (1), 195–245. www.hbs.edu/ris/Publication%20 Files/Imprinting2013_d39bb540-95ab-49c2-b6ce-cfa069ced663.pdf (archived at https://perma.cc/F4FC-ARD2)

2 B Franklin (1789/1907) Letter to Jean-Baptiste Le Roy, 13 November 1789, *The Writings of Benjamin Franklin*, ed Albert Henry Smyth, vol 10, Macmillan, 1907, 69–70.

3 WEF, Future of jobs 2023: These are the most in-demand skills now – and beyond, WEF, 2023. https://www.weforum.org/stories/2023/05/future-of-jobs-2023-skills/ (archived at https://perma.cc/KH6S-7RKK)

4 WEF, The Future of Jobs Report 2023, WEF, 2023. https://www.weforum.org/publications/the-future-of-jobs-report-2023/digest/ (archived at https://perma.cc/4AB4-X58J)

5 S E Chang, A Y Liu and S Lin. Exploring privacy and trust for employee monitoring, *Industrial Management and Data Systems*, 2015, 115 (1), 88–106. doi.org/10.1108/IMDS-07-2014-0197 (archived at https://perma.cc/X3ZL-3WZ7)

6 M Lerner. Electronically monitoring your employees? It's impacting their mental health, APA, 2023. www.apa.org/topics/healthy-workplaces/employee-electronic-monitoring (archived at https://perma.cc/2GXH-G9YE)

7 J van Wingerden, A B Bakker and D Derks. The longitudinal impact of a job crafting intervention, *European Journal of Work and Organizational Psychology*, 2017, 26 (1), 107–19. www.tandfonline.com/doi/full/10.1080/1359432X.2016.1224233 (archived at https://perma.cc/TB54-NLDB)

8 E L Deci and R M Ryan (1985) *Intrinsic Motivation and Self-Determination in Human Behavior*, Springer.

9 B M McKimmie. Cognitive dissonance theory, Springer Nature, 2020. doi.org/10.1007/978-3-319-24612-3_1121 (archived at https://perma.cc/MH4F-H8ZA)

10 E Seppälä (2016) *The Happiness Track: How to apply the science of happiness to accelerate your success*, HarperOne.

11 BambooHR. The great gloom: In 2023, employees are unhappier than ever. Why? BambooHR, 2023. www.bamboohr.com/resources/data-at-work/employee-happiness-index/q2-2023-the-great-gloom (archived at https://perma.cc/5FSU-6Q9P)

12 Global Wellness Institute. The global wellness economy reaches a record $5.6 trillion – and it's forecast to hit $8.5 trillion by 2027, Global Wellness Institute, 2023. globalwellnessinstitute.org/press-room/press-releases/globalwellnesseconomymonitor2023 (archived at https://perma.cc/D7CZ-G2BU)

13 Fortune Business Insights. Corporate wellness market, Fortune Business Insights, 2023. www.fortunebusinessinsights.com/corporate-wellness-market-106931 (archived at https://perma.cc/X6ZN-232R)

14 W J Fleming. Employee wellbeing outcomes from individual-level mental health interventions: Cross-sectional evidence from the United Kingdom, *Industrial Relations Journal*, 2024, 55 (2), 162–85.

15 E Perry. What is altruism (and is it important at work)? BetterUp, 2021. www.betterup.com/blog/altruism (archived at https://perma.cc/V64S-SVEH)

16 Canadian Museum for Human Rights. The story of Nelson Mandela, Canadian Museum for Human Rights, 2018. humanrights.ca/story/story-nelson-mandela (archived at https://perma.cc/4JQE-NBQ2)

17 J Brooke. Mandela visits apartheid die-hards, *The New York Times*, 1995. www.nytimes.com/1995/08/16/world/mandela-visits-apartheid-die-hards.html (archived at https://perma.cc/8J5L-YL8S)

18 J Brooke. Mandela visits apartheid die-hards, *The New York Times*, 1995. www.nytimes.com/1995/08/16/world/mandela-visits-apartheid-die-hards.html (archived at https://perma.cc/8J5L-YL8S)

19 B Baker. A four-decade secret: One man's story of sabotaging Carter's re-election, *The New York Times*, 2023. www.nytimes.com/2023/03/18/us/politics/jimmy-carter-october-surprise-iran-hostages.html (archived at https://perma.cc/8FZ8-7X8R)

20 L McGinley. How Jimmy Carter boosted a life-saving cancer drug, *The Washington Post*, 2023. www.washingtonpost.com/health/2023/03/06/jimmy-carter-melanoma-cancer-immune-therapy (archived at https://perma.cc/59AH-S44T)

8

Lessons on how to build a truly caring company

We talk a lot about culture these days – how to define it, shape it and scale it. But, if there's one thing I believe, it's that a truly caring culture is the foundation of everything we do. When people feel genuinely cared for, they show up differently; they're engaged, loyal and even energized. For companies aiming to make care the heart of their culture, H&R Block provides a powerful case study on what scaling care looks like in action – from employees to customers and the broader community.

Why should caring be on our radar now, more than ever? Simple. Workplaces have changed drastically, and the expectations of employees and customers alike have shifted. I will reiterate – people don't just want a job or a brand to buy from, they're looking for purpose, trust and empathy. A culture of care meets this need, making a real impact on everyone involved.

Let's start with the big question: why care? Why does it matter so much?

In today's work environment, people want to know they're valued beyond their roles. Employees want workplaces where they're not only respected but also supported through all stages of life.

According to O.C. Tanner's 2025 Global Culture Study, 'the degree to which employees believe their organization cares about them has a dramatic impact on their perception of whether they're thriving at work'. Their research found that employees who had a 'strong sense the organization cares about me' showed a 378 per cent increase in self-reported 'thriving at work'. When you compared the data to those who had a 'weak sense the organization cares about me' it was startling. Sense of thriving was reduced by 80 per cent.[1]

But caring is more than a marketing strategy or a line on the 'About us' page. It's about how we treat people, day in and day out.

H&R Block

H&R Block's journey offers us a roadmap for making this happen on a meaningful scale.

Step 1: Leading through life stages

In 2021, H&R Block reimagined their benefits, introducing a programme that addresses the diverse realities employees face, from family planning to mental health support, to parental and caregiving leave. For example, their inclusive benefits package includes resources for neurodiverse individuals and extensive support for family planning, including adoption and surrogacy assistance. It's a far cry from the traditional benefits package. And it sends a strong message: 'We see you. We understand your journey, and we're here to support you.'

Think about the impact this has on a person's commitment to their workplace. When a company acknowledges and supports the complexities of life, it fosters a deep sense of loyalty and belonging. If we want our organizations to be places people love working at, this kind of holistic care is non-negotiable.

We're finally talking more about mental health, but how many companies are genuinely acting on it? H&R Block's mental health initiatives go beyond simply providing resources. They've integrated mental health awareness into their everyday practices, offering coaching and resources to help employees manage stress, build resilience and feel supported. They've made it clear that mental well-being is as essential as physical health, breaking down the stigma and making space for these conversations.

If you're wondering how to bring more care into your company, here's a thought: start by making mental health visible, accessible and supported. In a world where burnout is rampant, showing that you care about people's mental health isn't just kind – it's essential.

Step 2: Flexibility shows trust

Caring means recognizing that life isn't a one-size-fits-all experience. One person's 'ideal workday' may be vastly different from another's. H&R Block gets this, which is why they've woven flexibility into their work model.

H&R Block's flexible work environment allows employees to balance office time with remote work. They ensure that working modes work well for all, and they listen and action when they don't. This shows employees that the company trusts them, values their judgement and respects their lives outside work. And when people feel trusted, they're more committed to the work they do.

One of H&R Block's most innovative programmes is The Annual Reboot. Every July, the entire company shuts down for a paid week off, giving everyone time to recharge. This isn't just a nice gesture; it sends a message that rest matters. For H&R Block, this initiative has translated to a refreshed, energized workforce ready to bring their best selves to work. And their employees love it.

Step 3: Recognize authentically

If there's one thing I believe strongly, it's that recognition is a powerful driver of happiness and fulfilment. People want to feel that their contributions matter, and that's why H&R Block has focused on personalized recognition.

Their programme, 'Best of Block Award', is a great example of this. Employees see this as a highly distinguished award. It's not about hitting some target; rather, it's a key milestone of H&R Block's recognition culture which, according to Tiffany Monroe, Chief People and Culture Officer at H&R Block, celebrates 'taking risks, acting boldly and solving tough problems in the spirit of bringing to life H&R Block's purpose: to provide help and inspire confidence in our clients and communities everywhere'.

If we want to scale a culture of care, recognition needs to be personal and value-driven. People need to know that their strengths are acknowledged in a way that feels authentic. This kind of care scales because it's genuine – it's about recognizing the individual impact within the larger organization.

Step 4: Care for the community

A truly caring company doesn't stop at its own walls. Scaling care means reaching out and making a positive impact on the world beyond the organization. H&R Block's approach to community care provides a model for what this looks like in practice.

Through the 'A Fair Shot' initiative, H&R Block supports gender equity by helping female college athletes secure fair name, image and likeness (NIL) deals. This isn't just about branding – it's about making a tangible difference on issues that matter to employees and customers alike. Community care initiatives like these show employees that they work for a company that stands for something larger than itself.

H&R Block also empowers employees to give back by matching donations to causes that matter to them. This approach not only supports the causes employees care about but also strengthens the connection they feel with their company. For companies aiming to scale care, encouraging employee-led philanthropy is a powerful way to foster a shared sense of purpose.

Why should companies care?

Caring companies aren't just idealistic; they're practical, resilient and increasingly essential in a competitive landscape.

- **For companies:** When companies build a caring culture, they see the payoff in retention, productivity and loyalty. Deloitte's research shows that prioritizing well-being reduces turnover by 57 per cent.[2] In a world where attracting and retaining talent is tough, caring companies have a clear advantage.
- **For employees:** When people feel cared for, they're more engaged, more fulfilled and more motivated. They bring their best selves to work. A caring culture reduces burnout, fosters loyalty and creates a workplace that people are excited to be a part of.
- **For customers and stakeholders:** Customers are becoming more selective about the brands they support. A culture of care not only attracts talent but builds customer loyalty. When consumers know a company genuinely cares about employees, the community and the planet, they're more likely to trust and support that brand.

Realistically, scaling a culture of care doesn't happen overnight. It's a continuous journey of listening, adapting, and showing up authentically. H&R Block's initiatives offer a powerful example of what's possible when care is woven into the very fabric of an organization.

Cisco

Cisco's culture of care: What it means to be number one in workplace well-being

Let's talk about what it really takes to be recognized as the top company for caring. In 2024, Cisco once again topped PEOPLE's '100 Companies That Care' list, which is no small feat. But here's what I find most fascinating:

Cisco didn't get there by following the usual playbook of perks and benefits. Instead, they've built a culture that's deeply rooted in social impact, inclusivity and true community involvement. So, how do they do it? And what does being number one on this list really mean?

Making it to the top of Great Place to Work and PEOPLE's Companies That Care list isn't just about having great policies on paper – it's about living those values in a way that resonates with employees and communities alike. The list itself considers factors like employee surveys, community engagement, social impact initiatives and an overall commitment to fostering an inclusive, compassionate workplace. For Cisco, it's clear that caring is part of their DNA, and that's why they continue to stand out in such a competitive field.

Step 1: Community care at the core

One of the things that sets Cisco apart is the scale of their social impact initiatives. They've made substantial investments in addressing critical issues like homelessness, committing over $130 million to fight housing insecurity. This isn't just a donation – it's a long-term commitment to improving the lives of people in the communities where they operate.

In 2018, Cisco decided to tackle homelessness in Santa Clara County. They pledged $50 million in grants over five years to achieve the following goals:

1. To make homelessness rare, brief and non-recurring in Santa Clara County.
2. To develop a replicable model for other regions beyond Silicon Valley.
3. To inspire other companies to join the fight against homelessness.

As of 2024, Cisco has invested over $130 million worldwide to address housing and homelessness going way beyond their original goal. They've focused mainly on supporting housing developments for people in need, homelessness prevention and making technology more accessible for underserved communities.

Cisco's commitment to homelessness goes beyond writing cheques. They partner with local organizations to support sustainable solutions, ensuring that their contributions lead to meaningful change. By taking bold steps to tackle social issues, they send a powerful message that companies can and should play a role in building better, more equitable communities.

Step 2: Giving time to give

A culture of care isn't just about what the company does – it's about empowering employees to make their own impact. Cisco's 'Time2Give' programme offers employees up to 80 hours of paid time off each year to volunteer for causes they're passionate about. This level of flexibility and support for personal philanthropy is rare, and it sends a clear message: caring isn't just encouraged, it's actively supported.

When employees are given the opportunity to volunteer, it creates a ripple effect. They feel connected not only to their communities but also to their colleagues who share similar values. Over 80 per cent of Cisco employees participate in community support activities, which is a testament to the culture Cisco has built. This high level of engagement amplifies the company's impact, extending its reach far beyond corporate headquarters and into the heart of the communities where employees live and work.

For other companies looking to scale care, this is a model worth emulating. Give people the time, resources and support they need to contribute to the causes they believe in. When employees feel that they're part of something bigger, their sense of loyalty and commitment grows stronger.

Step 3: Fostering a culture of belonging

Inclusivity is a huge part of Cisco's culture of care. In fact, they don't just talk about inclusion – they operationalize it in ways that genuinely make a difference.

One of Cisco's unique approaches to inclusivity is their requirement that any partner organization receiving social impact funding must ensure that at least 65 per cent of the programme participants come from underrepresented or vulnerable groups. This policy demonstrates Cisco's commitment to inclusivity not only within their walls but across their extended network. They're using their influence and resources to drive equity in the communities they touch, setting a new standard for corporate responsibility.

For employees, working for a company that champions inclusivity in such a tangible way enhances their sense of purpose and pride. Cisco's message is clear: inclusion isn't just an internal policy; it's a promise to everyone they work with.

Internally, Cisco also foster an environment where diversity is celebrated and psychological safety is a priority. Cisco's culture emphasizes open communication and respect, creating a space where employees feel comfortable bringing their whole selves to work. This isn't just a feel-good measure – studies show that when employees feel safe to express themselves, they're more innovative, engaged and collaborative.

Step 4: Scaling care by scaling trust

One of the reasons Cisco's culture of care works so well is because it's built on transparency and trust. They regularly communicate with employees about the impact of their social initiatives, share the outcomes of community projects and even disclose how funds are allocated in various programmes.

Cisco's leaders hold regular 'Ask Me Anything' sessions, where employees can submit questions and get real, unfiltered answers. This open-door policy isn't just a formality; it's a powerful tool for building trust. When employees feel they have a direct line to leaders, it creates a sense of transparency and security that enhances their connection to the company. In a world where corporate intentions are often questioned, Cisco's commitment to transparency makes a statement: we're here for you, and we want you to know exactly how we're making a difference together.

Cisco also actively share stories of the impact they're making, from community housing projects to individual volunteer stories. By highlighting these contributions, Cisco reminds employees that their work is part of something larger. This storytelling approach reinforces the company's purpose and shows that every team member plays a role in Cisco's mission to build a better world. I've mentioned how important storytelling is for organizational success. Sharing impact stories can be an effective way to bring meaning to the everyday tasks that employees complete, connecting their roles to a bigger picture.

Cisco's high retention rates and employee engagement scores are a testament to the loyalty and dedication that a caring culture fosters. When employees feel supported and empowered to make an impact, they're more engaged, creative and resilient.

From significant community investments to empowering employees through volunteer programmes, they've created a workplace where caring is not just encouraged – it happens at Cisco's. Topping PEOPLE's '100 Companies That Care' list is more than an accolade for Cisco; it's a reflection of their commitment to building a better world, inside and outside their organization.

Lessons for leaders: Unlocking happiness at work through a culture of care

If you want a game-changing employee retention strategy, consider a culture of care. The kind of care that shows up in real ways, that say, 'You matter.' Companies like H&R Block and Cisco have figured out how to make care the cornerstone of their cultures, and the results speak for themselves. By putting people first, they've unlocked something many leaders are still searching for: genuine happiness at work.

H&R Block reminds us that real care means seeing people beyond their job titles. Their benefits, like flexible work options and comprehensive support for life's ups and downs, show us what it looks like to meet employees where they are. It's a simple but profound lesson: if we want our teams to feel valued, we have to support them as whole people. When we believe our company has our back in and out of the office, it's a lot easier to show up with energy and commitment.

For leaders, this is a reminder to build policies and benefits that resonate with real lives. Happiness grows in environments where people don't feel like they have to leave parts of themselves at the door. It's about creating space for their families, their mental health, their passions – all the things that make them who they are.

Cisco takes care to another level by giving employees a sense of purpose. Through programmes like 'Time2Give' and their dedication to fighting homelessness, they've woven community impact into the fabric of their organization. When people know their work contributes to something meaningful, it transforms how they feel about coming to work each day. Purpose becomes the spark that makes a job feel less like a job and more like a mission.

If there's a takeaway here, it's that leaders should look for ways to connect their teams to something bigger. It could be encouraging volunteerism or aligning work with causes that resonate. Purpose doesn't have to be some grand thing – it's about helping people feel that what they do matters. And from what I've seen, when people believe in the mission, they bring their best selves forward.

Both H&R Block and Cisco also get that trust is the foundation of any strong workplace. Cisco's regular 'Ask Me Anything' sessions and H&R Block's inclusive policies aren't just good HR practices, they're acts of care that say, 'We value your voice.' When we're transparent, when we include everyone in the conversation, we build a community where people feel safe and respected.

For leaders, this means opening up the dialogue. Let people in on the 'why' behind decisions. Make inclusivity more than a buzzword by ensuring that policies truly reflect the diversity of experiences in your team. Happiness isn't just about perks – it's about creating a culture where people feel they belong, where they feel heard and respected.

I've seen the research, but, more importantly, I've seen the impact care has on people's lives. When you care, people stick around. They engage. They thrive.

HAPPINESS IN ACTION

Changing the world is hard. If we want to have big goals, we need to be open to criticism and comfortable with iterating on our strategies. Ego in leadership can be highly destructive. In the stories above, the greatest examples of strong leadership rose out of humility, criticism and openness to learning. These two activities offer training on how to let go of strategies that aren't working for us and learn the reasons why they didn't work to avoid repeating them.

Letting go

Although it's useful to focus on the strategies that are effective in helping us get through difficult times, analysing the coping strategies that weren't effective or beneficial can be just as important. Sometimes leaving a strategy behind is the best way to move forward because the more effective your problem-solving strategies are, the better you can overcome hurdles.

1. List and describe two strategies you've tried in the past that weren't useful, or that were perhaps even detrimental.
2. Now, reflect on those two events and analyse what coping mechanisms ended up being more successful.
3. Write down what made those strategies effective vs the others that weren't as effective.

Shifting narratives for change readiness

We all experience challenges in our life. Changing the way we think about challenging situations can help to protect us against negative emotions, and the stress associated with those feelings. It can also make us less prone to disappointment and able to recover faster when we inevitably bump up against challenging times again in the future. It may be difficult to see the positives while we are buried in stress, but with practice and building up our psychological fitness we become more cognisant of the positives around us.

1. To start, describe one low point you've experienced in the past.
2. Now, imagine that you have to look at this event with gratitude. That may seem challenging, for some of you even impossible, but start off simple. Begin by imagining a positive in your life now that would not have existed if this event hadn't occurred.
3. As you watch your list of benefits grow, you can begin reframing that challenge into an opportunity.

This activity can be attached to any challenging or stressful event. Over time, you can reframe most of your negative memories. Although it doesn't mean that your stress wasn't real or shouldn't be acknowledged, it just changes whether it will continue to have a negative impact on your present and future self.

HAPPY LEARNING!

Read

- Mycoskie, B (2012) *Start Something that Matters*, Spiel & Grau
- Tan, C-M, Goleman, D and Kabat-Zinn, J (2012) *Search Inside Yourself: The unexpected path to achieving success, happiness (and world peace)*, HarperOne

Watch

- Edmondson, A (2014) Building a psychologically safe workspace, TED/YouTube. www.youtube.com/watch?v=LhoLuui9gX8

Notes

1. O C Tanner. Thriving at work, O C Tanner, 2025. www.octanner.com/global-culture-report/2025-thriving-at-work (archived at https://perma.cc/8RXN-F6WA)
2. Workplace Intelligence, C-suite's role in well-being study, 2022. workplaceintelligence.com/c-suites-role-in-well-being-study (archived at https://perma.cc/4Y47-S5N7)

9

The history of happiness

Before we dive into the next and final chapter, 'The future of happiness' – where we investigate the exciting and sometimes shocking innovations happening today – let's jump back in time for a moment. To fully understand why the well-being industry continues to evolve is to understand the history of happiness, which is vast, deep and winding.

There are not enough pages in this chapter, or chapters in this book, to cover the entire history of the happiness timeline. To solve this (and to ensure relevancy) we're going to walk through some of what I deem to be the most interesting milestones in the evolution of happiness – with a focus on workplace and leadership.

In recent years, the conversation around happiness has shifted dramatically, fuelled by a growing recognition that it's not just a personal pursuit but also a societal one. The way we think about happiness today is far more nuanced than in the past, influenced by advancements in neuroscience, psychology and social science.

Thinkers like Arthur Brooks, whose *Atlantic* article 'The American pursuit of happiness' sparked discussions on how material success often fails to translate into long-term contentment.[1]

Researchers like Sonja Lyubomirsky and Martin Seligman, pioneers in the field of positive psychology, have reframed happiness as something that can be cultivated intentionally rather than merely sought after. I dig deeper into Lyubomirsky and Seligman's work later in the chapter, but particularly Seligman's book *Authentic Happiness*[2] laid the groundwork for understanding happiness not just as fleeting pleasure but as deep fulfilment tied to purpose, meaning and relationships. These thought leaders have encouraged a shift away from viewing happiness as a static state to be achieved and towards seeing it as a dynamic process that can be nurtured through specific actions and mind-sets.

Happiness is not just a personal matter; it's also essential in the workplace, where it plays a critical role in driving engagement, productivity and overall well-being. In fact, the modern focus on happiness has reshaped how we view employee satisfaction and organizational success. Thought leaders like Shawn Achor, author of *The Happiness Advantage*, have popularized the idea that happiness fuels success, not the other way around. His research shows that happy employees are more creative, resilient and collaborative, leading to better outcomes for both individuals and organizations. When happiness is prioritized, it activates the brain's reward system, boosting motivation and fostering prosocial behaviours, like cooperation and trust, that are key to a thriving workplace culture.[3]

As we explore the history of happiness, it's clear that this conversation has evolved – from the classical notions of virtue and well-being espoused by ancient philosophers, to today's more scientific understanding of how happiness works in the brain and in our lives. This chapter will explore how modern thinkers and experts have redefined happiness, positioning it as a cornerstone for both individual fulfilment and societal progress.

Socrates

Socrates, the Greek philosopher, was a rule-breaker and a rebel, and the person who would be recognized for advancing conversations related to happiness and the meaning of life. Socrates was also one of the first to openly debate whether happiness is in our control.

Socrates' inevitable downfall was owing to the timing of his theories during an era that was not friendly to any concepts that opposed the Greek gods. In 480 BCE when Socrates was espousing his theories of happiness, the Greeks were not only pessimistic about humans and their lack of capacity for greatness, they also believed that joy was only reserved for those chosen as worthy by the gods.

If the gods had cared to listen some 2,400 years ago, they would have learned that Socrates was attempting to suggest, through scientific thinking, that to achieve happiness we all should consider the following tenets:

1. Strive for honesty.
2. Be your best possible self.
3. Demonstrate emotional control.

These tenets also happen to be key traits of high-performing and effective leaders. The type of leaders to help their employees unlock happiness at work.

Socrates also developed the Socratic method, which involves asking and answering questions to stimulate critical thinking. At its core, the Socratic method encourages self-reflection and self-examination, prompting individuals to question their beliefs, values and assumptions. This process of introspection can lead to greater self-awareness, which is a key component of happiness. By engaging in deep reflection, people are more likely to align their actions with their true values and purpose, leading to a more fulfilling and meaningful life.

Furthermore, the Socratic method helps individuals uncover cognitive distortions or irrational beliefs, which are often at the root of unhappiness. Through questioning, one can challenge negative thought patterns, similar to techniques used in cognitive behavioural therapy. By questioning these thoughts – much like Socrates questioned his peers – individuals can reframe them in a way that promotes emotional well-being and reduces anxiety or stress.

In the context of work and personal life, the Socratic method also fosters prosocial behaviours by encouraging curiosity and understanding rather than judgement. When applied to dialogue within teams or relationships, it promotes openness, empathy and constructive problem-solving, which are all factors that contribute to a harmonious, happier environment.

Unfortunately, in the end Socrates paid heavily for his public commentary and efforts to prove that happiness was a choice and not handed down from the gods. He was convicted of 'corrupting the youth' and sentenced to die by hemlock poisoning.

And yet, in those last few minutes before he died, instead of ruminating on his pain and blaming the gods for their misguided punishment or begging for mercy, Socrates was jovial with his friend Plato and others. He reminded them about his teachings and assuaged them of their fears. He would be remembered as happy, right up until the moment he drank the poison.

Socrates is elemental to the topic of happiness through history because he lived as he believed. Socrates was so entirely committed to the concept that happiness is a choice that he wanted to have it validated even just moments before his death.

Aristotle

After Socrates, Aristotle is one of the most significant figures in early history to advance the conversation about happiness. In his work, *Nicomachean Ethics*, Aristotle introduced the concept of *eudaimonia*, often translated as 'happiness' or 'flourishing'. However, Aristotle's view of happiness went beyond simple pleasure or momentary joy. For him, happiness was about living a life of virtue and excellence in accordance with reason.

Aristotle argued that true happiness comes from fulfilling one's potential and living in harmony with one's highest self, a state achieved through the cultivation of virtues such as courage, wisdom and temperance. He believed that happiness was not a passive experience but an active pursuit, requiring effort and moral character. This idea of happiness as a life-long process of self-improvement and alignment with one's purpose has influenced many modern theories of well-being and personal fulfilment.

Aristotle came up with the concept of the 'Golden Mean', which he used to explain how moderation leads to true happiness. Aristotle believed that living virtuously meant finding a balance between extremes. For example, courage is a virtue, but it lies between the extremes of rashness and cowardice.

Aristotle's teachings on happiness and the Golden Mean deeply influenced Alexander the Great during their time together, especially in areas of self-control and moderation. While Aristotle emphasized the importance of balance and avoiding excess in all aspects of life, this lesson was crucial for Alexander, who was known for his ambitions and larger-than-life conquests. Interestingly, during their time together, Aristotle did more than just teach philosophy – he integrated lessons about governance, ethics and self-restraint, which would later be visible in Alexander's leadership style.

However, I'm sure we can all agree that, despite Aristotle's teachings on moderation, Alexander's relentless drive for conquest and power often clashed with the idea of the Golden Mean. We only have to point to the story of Cleitus the Black. After he'd openly accused him of dishonouring his father's legacy, Alexander seized a spear and fatally struck his best friend who'd saved his life many times in battle. This would become a turning point for Alexander and shows us that there always exists tension between theory and practice in life. Almost immediately after realizing what he had done, Alexander was filled with immense guilt and grief. Accounts suggest that he fell into deep despair, isolating himself for days and repeatedly expressing regret over killing one of his oldest and most loyal companions.

Imagine the result of his leadership without Aristotle's influence.

William James

William James was Professor of Psychology and Philosophy at Harvard University and became one of the most famous living American psychologists and philosophers of his time.

James shared in his *Principles of Psychology* (1890)[4] the idea that involuntary reactions come first – like a baby swallowing air for the first time and then later feeding. Or, when a baby is hungry and cries to be fed. When a child develops a memory to supersede their instinct, it moves to a conscious decision the next time it chooses to cry for food.

Now this is where it gets interesting.

James believed that when a memory is formed and we can select it as a choice then this is when free will develops in our psyche. Happiness becomes something in our memory to act on or ignore and we can then direct the flow of emotional traffic appropriately.

What is most provocative about this discovery is that James was able to explain how happiness is partially innate (built into our genetic makeup) and yet a large part of happiness is dependent on whether we want to incorporate it into our narratives or ignore it (learned and chosen). James famously stated, 'The art of being wise is the art of knowing what to overlook'.

Going back to the nature vs nurture argument (our genes vs our developed understanding), William James established a term for each. He described people as Once Born and Twice Born.

Once Born people are those who seem to be biologically predisposed to happiness while Twice Born people are born with a natural pessimism.

You'd naturally assume that the Twice Born are less happy, but James believed that crisis is often followed by a born or innate desire to make sense of things and because a negative emotional state impedes us from finding resolution, we are forced to 'rise above' our circumstances.[5]

Essentially, having more experience with a range of emotions – even ones that can feel unpleasant and can make us pessimistic – is how we find true happiness in the end.

One of his most influential ideas related to happiness is found in his work on pragmatism. James argued that the truth of an idea should be judged by its practical consequences. When applied to happiness, this means that the beliefs and actions that lead to practical well-being are what matter most. Happiness, according to James, isn't about abstract ideals but rather about finding beliefs that foster well-being in real life.[6]

James also highlighted the role of attitude in achieving happiness, most notably in his concept of 'the will to believe' which he outlined in his book of the same name. He emphasized that individuals have the power to choose beliefs and actions that promote optimism and happiness, even when faced with uncertainty. This idea echoes in modern-day concepts of positive psychology, where focusing on positive thinking and resilience is seen as a key component of well-being.[7]

In his work *The Varieties of Religious Experience*, James explored how different spiritual and emotional experiences contribute to a sense of fulfilment and happiness. He believed that emotional well-being, or happiness, could be cultivated through both spiritual practices and practical, everyday actions.[8]

What is special about William James within the happiness history timeline is how he advanced the conversation about happiness by connecting it to practical action, the power of belief and emotional resilience. His integration of philosophy and psychology continues to influence modern ideas about how we can create meaning and happiness in our lives.

Abraham Maslow

After William James, one of the most influential figures in the history of happiness is Abraham Maslow (1908–70). Maslow, a psychologist, revolutionized the understanding of happiness with his Hierarchy of Needs Theory, which positioned happiness and self-fulfilment as essential elements of human motivation. His model depicted a pyramid where basic physiological and safety needs form the foundation, while higher-level needs – like love, esteem and self-actualization – culminate in the experience of well-being and happiness.[9]

Maslow's work was pioneering in the sense that it connected happiness to self-actualization, which he described as the fulfilment of personal potential. According to Maslow, only once a person's more basic needs (such as food, shelter and safety) are met can they pursue higher-level psychological needs that lead to true happiness and fulfilment. He suggested that individuals achieve happiness by realizing their potential, being creative and finding purpose in their lives.

Maslow's ideas laid the groundwork for later developments in positive psychology, particularly by scholars like Martin Seligman, who further explored the link between personal strengths and happiness. Maslow helped broaden the conversation about happiness by shifting the focus from external circumstances (like wealth or material success) to inner development and personal growth.

Maslow's focus on human potential and personal growth continues to inform workplace well-being programmes, educational philosophies and therapeutic practices centred on achieving greater fulfilment and happiness.

In my research and work on preventing stress – a barrier to happiness at work – I frequently draw on Frederick Herzberg's Two-Factor Hygiene-Motivation theory, which he developed under the influence of Abraham Maslow. Herzberg's theory divides workplace factors into two categories: hygiene factors and motivators. Hygiene factors, such as salary, job security and working conditions, are necessary to prevent dissatisfaction.[10]

Frederick Herzberg and Abraham Maslow were contemporaries and shared many overlapping ideas, and were both instrumental in advancing the conversation related to motivation and well-being.

Edward Deci and Richard Ryan

We discussed Deci and Ryan's Self-Determination Theory (SDT) in Chapter 7; to quickly recap, their theory emphasizes that the key to happiness at work isn't just about external rewards (like salary or benefits) but about meeting intrinsic psychological needs like autonomy, competence and relatedness.[11]

A great example of Edward Deci and Richard Ryan's research on SDT comes from their famous Soma Puzzle experiment in the 1970s, which highlighted the tension between intrinsic and extrinsic motivation.

Here's how it went: Deci invited college students into the lab to play with a 3D puzzle called the Soma Puzzle – a bit like a physical version of Tetris. The students were told to solve as many puzzles as they liked during the session. However, one group was paid for each puzzle they completed (extrinsic motivation), while the other group wasn't offered any money (relying on intrinsic motivation – their internal enjoyment of the activity).[12]

Now, the twist came when Deci left the room, leaving the students alone with the puzzles. The group that wasn't paid kept playing, happily solving puzzles simply for the enjoyment of the activity. But the group that had been paid? Once the money stopped, their interest dropped dramatically, and they stopped playing as much.

This study was one of the first to show that rewards can backfire by undermining intrinsic motivation. Essentially, when people are rewarded externally for something they might already enjoy (like solving a fun puzzle or doing creative work), the reward can strip away their natural enjoyment of the task. This finding was groundbreaking because it challenged the traditional belief that people are always motivated by external rewards like money or prizes.

This experiment has huge implications for workplace culture – especially today when new research shows that many people are willing to trade higher salaries for more meaningful work. The 2024 Deloitte *Gen Z and Millennial Survey* found that, on average, these cohorts would be willing to sacrifice up to 23 per cent of their lifetime earnings to work in roles that provide deeper meaning.[13] This willingness to accept lower pay for greater job satisfaction is part of a broader trend where employees prioritize purpose, well-being and work/life balance over monetary compensation.

Deci and Ryan's research shows that if leaders rely too heavily on external rewards (bonuses, salary rises, etc) they may actually demotivate employees over time. Instead, focusing on autonomy (letting employees have control over their work), competence (helping them feel skilled), and relatedness (creating strong social connections) fosters intrinsic motivation. And that's where real, sustained happiness and engagement come from.

In essence, Deci and Ryan showed us that genuine motivation isn't bought – it's cultivated from within.

Martin Seligman

The next major figure in the conversation about happiness, particularly as it relates to workplace well-being, is Martin Seligman, who developed Positive Psychology. Building on the work of Deci and Ryan's Self-Determination Theory, Seligman focused on flourishing and well-being rather than just the absence of mental illness.

I had the privilege of getting to know Martin Seligman during my time on the Global Happiness and Well-being Council and in the writing of my book, *Why Are We Here?* He is a kind and thoughtful person and I was honoured and humbled to spend time with him.

In one of our encounters, he shared exciting new insights from his latest joint project, *Tomorrowmind*, a book he co-wrote with Dr Gabriella Rosen

Kellerman, Harvard-trained MD and Chief Innovation Officer at virtual coaching platform BetterUp.[14]

'More than a hundred years ago when psychology and psychiatry began, the interest was in misery and suffering, and pathology,' he told me. 'Freud told us all that the best we could ever do in life was not to be miserable, not to suffer, to hold our suffering as close to zero as possible. It was my privilege when I became president of the American Psychological Association to say to my fellow members, "This is half baked",' Seligman said.

He went on to explain that now there are different fields where one is still there to help reduce misery and suffering but there now exists another field that focuses on the science of measuring and building peak performance. 'What makes life worth living, not just what purpose of life,' Seligman shares.

Seligman is responsible for defining the term 'PERMA', the root of many positive psychology research projects around the world. The acronym stands for the five elements essential to lasting contentment (Figure 9.1):

P – Positive emotion: Peace, gratitude, satisfaction, pleasure, inspiration, hope, curiosity and love fall into this category. Distinguishing between pleasure and enjoyment is a central consideration. Pleasure is connected to sustaining bodily needs such as thirst, hunger and sleep. Enjoying a moment or a series of moments comes from intellectual stimulation and creativeness.

E – Engagement: Losing ourselves to a task or project that provides us with a sense of 'disappeared time' because we are so highly engaged. When we are passionate about the work we're engrossed in, it can create a sense of 'flow' or 'bliss'. This feeling can occur in our extracurricular pursuits, from dancing to exercising to gardening. It can also occur at work. As the saying goes, 'If you love what you do, you'll never work a day in your life.'

R – Relationships: People who have meaningful, positive relationships with others are happier than those who do not. Since we spend 70 per cent of our waking hours at work, it becomes even more important for us as leaders to facilitate those healthy, positive relationships.

M – Meaning: Meaning comes from serving a cause bigger than ourselves. Whether a religion or a cause that helps humanity in some way, we all need meaning in our lives. When we build in meaning at work for our employees, it creates a deeper sense of accomplishment when goals are

FIGURE 9.1 The PERMA model

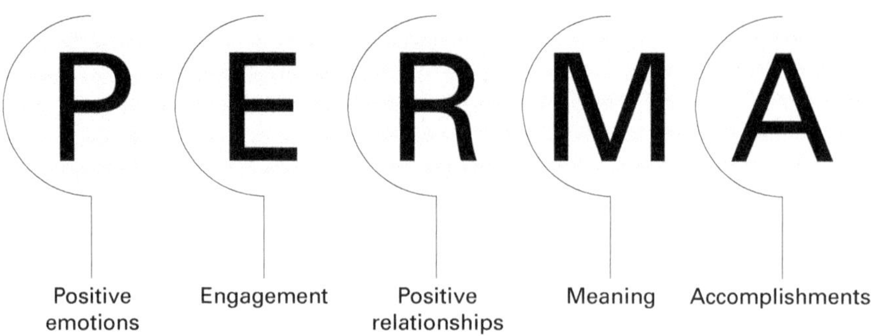

reached. We then attach value to their input, which leads to a happier, healthier work experience.

A – Accomplishment/achievement: To feel significant life satisfaction, we must strive to better ourselves in some way. We tend to only focus on the home runs or the big goals instead of celebrating the small wins that take us to those big goals. When we break down the effort, we can feel like we're on the path to success, versus pursuing a distant goal.

The PERMA model reminds us that happiness is not about chasing pleasure, but rather actively engaging in long-term, sustainable life goals that include daily investments in positive work, activities and relationships.

In recent years, Seligman's PERMA model has evolved and expanded to include more nuanced aspects of well-being, particularly in workplace and educational settings. The original five elements of PERMA – positive emotions, engagement, relationships, meaning, and accomplishment – remain central to understanding human flourishing, but researchers and practitioners have added new layers of understanding to these concepts.

First, Seligman has proposed a subtle shift in his PERMA model, particularly in the element of 'meaning', where he now favours the term 'mattering' in some contexts. He emphasizes that feeling like you matter – to others, to your community or within your work – is a core component of well-being. Mattering emphasizes personal significance and social impact, suggesting that people not only need to find meaning in what they do but also need to feel that they are making a difference and are valued by those around them.

This shift mirrors ongoing research into the importance of psychological safety, recognition and belonging in the workplace and other social environments.

Seligman's work is essential in modern approaches to employee engagement and well-being because it emphasizes the importance of meaning and purpose – key drivers of motivation and happiness, which aligns with the previous work by Deci and Ryan on intrinsic motivation. His focus on well-being and flourishing has become a cornerstone in workplace culture initiatives that aim to enhance productivity, creativity and resilience by fostering a positive work environment.

Continuing the happiness conversation

A number of key figures are advancing the conversation on happiness and well-being today. One of them is Daniel Kahneman, a psychologist and Nobel laureate, who passed away in 2024. Kahneman contributed significantly to the happiness discussion through his research on decision-making and well-being. We've discussed his work throughout the book; his research has had a profound impact on the world that continues to this day. Particularly in his book *Thinking, Fast and Slow*, he sheds light on the cognitive biases that affect how we perceive happiness. Kahneman introduced the concepts of experienced well-being (how we feel in the moment) and remembered well-being (how we evaluate our overall life satisfaction). He highlights the idea that people often misjudge what will make them happy, leading to decisions that don't always maximize happiness.[15]

He also pioneered the concept of the 'Peak End Rule' which discovered that when participants were subjected to unpleasant experiences those who had a painful experience that ended gently remembered the experience more positively than those with shorter but more intensely painful procedures, showing that our most recent memory of the experience is what stays with us.[16]

Brené Brown is a researcher and author known for her work on vulnerability, courage and emotional well-being. Her research has highlighted the importance of authenticity and emotional resilience in achieving happiness and fulfilment. In *Daring Greatly: How the courage to be vulnerable transforms the way we live, love, parent, and lead*, Brown discusses how vulnerability, often seen as a weakness, can be a superpower for innovation. She found that teams where members were comfortable admitting mistakes and expressing uncertainty had a better capacity to innovate. In environments where employees felt safe being vulnerable, they were more likely to take risks and come up with bold, creative solutions.[17]

Michelle Gielan is a former national CBS News anchor turned positive psychology researcher. She authored *Broadcasting Happiness* and focuses on how optimism and positive communication can transform workplaces. Gielan's work on broadcasting happiness uncovered the transformative power of positive messaging. In one study, employees who received positive, solution-focused communication from their leaders reported a 31 per cent increase in productivity. Moreover, teams exposed to this positive leadership style experienced a dramatic boost in morale and engagement, reshaping the way organizations think about the role of communication in productivity.[18]

You've already been introduced to Emma Seppälä, Science Director at Stanford University's Center for Compassion and Altruism Research and Education. She has conducted extensive research on the relationship between compassion, well-being and success. Seppälä argues that focusing on happiness and emotional resilience is essential for personal and professional success, and she promotes mindfulness and compassion as key tools for thriving in work environments.

Seppälä's research on breathing techniques showed that something as simple as controlled breathing could rewire the brain for resilience. In one study, she found that participants who practised slow, deep breathing for just five minutes a day experienced a significant drop in the stress hormone cortisol and increased activity in the pre-frontal cortex, the brain's centre for decision-making and emotional regulation. This technique was shown to boost well-being and make people more effective at handling stress. Her research on yoga-based breathing for military veterans with trauma was highlighted in the documentary *Free the Mind*.[19]

A pioneer in the field of positive psychology, Sonja Lyubomirsky is best known for her book *The How of Happiness*, which breaks down the science of happiness into actionable steps. Her research suggests that 40 per cent of our happiness is within our control – based on our actions and thoughts – rather than being fixed by genetics or circumstances. She has become a major voice in understanding how happiness can be cultivated and how it impacts our everyday lives, especially in high-stress environments like the workplace.[20]

One of Lyubomirsky's well-known studies involved participants performing acts of kindness over the course of several weeks. In this experiment, participants were asked to perform five acts of kindness per week for six weeks. The results showed that engaging in these prosocial behaviours significantly increased participants' overall well-being. Moreover, it was found that those who varied their acts of kindness – rather than repeating the same acts – experienced a greater boost in happiness. This study highlighted the power of generosity and variety in creating lasting happiness.

Dr Laurie Santos, a Yale University professor, has been leading the charge in popularizing the science of happiness through her famous course, The Science of Well-being, and her podcast, The Happiness Lab. Her research emphasizes how understanding cognitive biases and behavioural science can help people make better choices to improve happiness and mental well-being. She is particularly known for showing how simple interventions can have profound effects on happiness.

For example, Santos describes the GI Joe fallacy – the idea that simply knowing what makes us happy is enough to change our behaviour. In her Science of Well-being course, Santos found that participants who actively practised happiness-boosting behaviours, like gratitude journaling and increasing social connections, saw immediate improvements in their well-being. Those who simply learned about these concepts but didn't apply them saw no change in happiness, proving that action is what truly drives long-term well-being.[21]

Shawn Achor is another major contributor to discussions related to workplace happiness today. Achor, who also wrote the Foreward for this book, is known for both his TED Talk, which is one of the most popular of all time with over 26 million views, and his bestselling book, *The Happiness Advantage*, where he argues that happiness fuels success, not the other way around. His work has built on positive psychology, particularly by applying these principles to the workplace and education. Achor's research focuses on how small, intentional changes in behaviour and mindset – like practising gratitude or developing resilience – can significantly improve happiness and, by extension, performance in professional and personal life.[22]

Achor's idea of the 'happiness advantage' demonstrates how positive thinking leads to more creativity, better problem-solving skills and increased sales, revenue and productivity. His work has been widely applied to corporate training programmes, helping leaders understand how fostering happiness can directly impact business outcomes.

In a study with tax auditors at KPMG, Achor introduced positive psychology interventions, such as writing down three things they were grateful for each day. After just 21 days, participants reported a 31 per cent increase in life satisfaction and a 19 per cent drop in stress levels, proving how small mindset shifts can create lasting happiness.

Achor continues to bridge the gap between positive psychology and real-world application, influencing how leaders think about well-being in modern work environments.

Angela Duckworth, Psychologist and Researcher at University of Pennsylvania, is responsible for popularizing the term 'grit'.[23] Her TED Talk on the subject has also been widely watched with 29 million views. Her research in Chicago schools found that kids were significantly more likely to graduate if they had higher grit, even when measured against things like family income and standardized achievement test scores.

Duckworth believes that the closest research to parallel the study of grit comes from Carol Dweck, Professor at Stanford University, who studies 'growth mindset', or the belief that the ability to learn is not fixed, that it can change with your effort. 'Dr Dweck has shown that when kids read and learn about the brain and how it changes and grows in response to challenge, they're much more likely to persevere when they fail, because they don't believe that failure is a permanent condition,' explains Duckworth.

Stories of business leaders like Howard Schulz, CEO of Starbucks, make us believe that we can achieve anything if we persevere. As a kid growing up poor in low-income housing, he saw his father break his leg at work, and without health insurance the family was financially devastated. This moment in time would live in Schulz's mind for decades – a catalyst for his own perseverance and desire to reduce vulnerability.

This concept of rebirth and redemption, and happiness as a result of trauma or crises, is a theme repeated throughout history, and Duckworth highlights how with adversity comes determination and a passion to succeed.

Another influential figure in this space today is Tal Ben-Shahar, who has popularized happiness research through his work as a lecturer at Harvard and as an author. Ben-Shahar combines insights from psychology, philosophy and management to create practical strategies for improving happiness in everyday life. His courses on happiness have gained global popularity, reinforcing the significance of well-being as a serious academic and corporate pursuit.

In his 'Hamburger Model' experiment, Ben-Shahar used a simple analogy of different hamburgers to demonstrate how people approach life's pleasures and challenges. He found that the happiest people choose the 'delayed gratification' hamburger – one that might not taste great in the short term (healthy lifestyle) but brings the most long-term happiness.[24]

Adam Grant, is a professor at Wharton, an organizational psychologist, and *New York Times* bestselling author of six books His ideas have influenced leadership strategies that focus on prosocial behaviours as a pathway to a more engaged and satisfied workforce.

In one fascinating experiment, Grant found that simply letting call centre workers listen to a student talk about how their scholarship funding changed their life led to a 400 per cent increase in worker productivity. This experiment showed that connecting people's work to a higher purpose can dramatically boost performance.[25]

In his 2023 book *Hidden Potential* he found that being open to new experiences can lead to unexpected breakthroughs. For instance, he shows how luck isn't purely random but can be 'manufactured' by preparing for unexpected opportunities – essentially, the more effort and preparation you invest, the more chances you create for serendipity to work in your favour.[26]

These luminaries continue to shape the evolving understanding of happiness, particularly how it can be cultivated in both personal and professional contexts today and in the future. The history of happiness is a journey through shifting perspectives, from the ancient Greeks' focus on virtue and moral living to the modern understanding of happiness as a psychological and societal goal.

Over time, people have shaped the narrative of happiness by shifting the focus from external factors, like wealth or status, to internal factors, such as purpose, relationships and psychological well-being. William James, a pioneer in psychology, helped advance the idea that happiness is tied to personal beliefs and actions, rather than circumstances, emphasizing the role of choice and mindset in cultivating well-being.

Today, researchers like Martin Seligman and Sonja Lyubomirsky have built on these ideas, showing that happiness can be intentionally nurtured through positive actions and interventions, further evolving our understanding of what it means to live a fulfilling life.

And, through the power of new technology and neurosciences research, happiness is something we can actively cultivate through small, consistent actions like gratitude, kindness and finding meaning in our work and relationships. The evolution of this concept shows how happiness has become not just an individual pursuit but a key driver of both personal fulfilment and collective well-being.

HAPPINESS IN ACTION

- Which luminary did you feel most connected to?
- If you could choose one happiness philosophy to embed in your organization which one would it be?
    - Define the strategy and come up with tactical ideas to test out with the team.
- Name something that your company is doing to advance happiness at work. How could you expand on it?

HAPPY LEARNING!

Read

- Ben-Shahar, T (2007) *Happier: Learn the secrets to daily joy and lasting fulfillment*, McGraw-Hill
- Brown, B (2012) *Daring Greatly: How the courage to be vulnerable transforms the way we live, love, parent, and lead*, Gotham Books
- Gielan, M (2015) *Broadcasting Happiness: The science of igniting and sustaining positive change*, BenBella Books
- Grant, A (2023) *Hidden Potential: The science of achieving greater things*, Viking
- Herzberg, F, Mausner, B and Bloch Snyderman, B (1959) *The Motivation to Work*, Wiley
- James, W (1890) *The Principles of Psychology*, Henry Holt
- Kahneman, D (2011) *Thinking, Fast and Slow*, Farrar, Straus and Giroux
- Kellerman, G and Seligman, M (2023) *Tomorrowmind: Thriving at work with resilience, creativity, and connection – now and in an uncertain future*, Atria Books
- Lyubomirsky, S (2008) *The How of Happiness: A new approach to getting the life you want*, Penguin Press
- Mandela, N (1995) *Long Walk to Freedom*, Back Bay Books
- Maslow, A (1954) *Motivation and Personality*, Harper & Row
- Seligman, M (2011) *Flourish: A visionary new understanding of happiness and well-being*, Nicholas Brealey Publishing

- Seppälä, E (2016) *The Happiness Track: How to apply the science of happiness to accelerate your success*, HarperOne

Watch

- Achor, S (2011) TEDxBloomington – Shawn Achor – 'The happiness advantage: Linking positive brains to performance', TED/YouTube. www.youtube.com/watch?v=GXy_kBVq1M (archived at https://perma.cc/85FS-8NYN)
- Duckworth, A (2013) The key to success? Grit, TED. ted.com/talks/angela_lee_duckworth_the_key_to_success_grit/transcript?language=en#t-181462 (archived at https://perma.cc/QL55-62LB)

Notes

1 A Brooks. The American pursuit of happiness, *The Atlantic*, 2021.
2 M E P Seligman (2002) *Authentic Happiness: Using the new positive psychology to realize your potential for lasting fulfillment*, Free Press.
3 S Achor (2010) *The Happiness Advantage: How a positive brain fuels success in work and life*, Crown Business.
4 W James (1890) *The Principles of Psychology*, Henry Holt.
5 W James (1902) *The Varieties of Religious Experience: A study in human nature*, Longmans, Green, and Co.
6 C Misak. Pragmatism, Stanford Encyclopedia of Philosophy, 2024. plato.stanford.edu/entries/pragmatism (archived at https://perma.cc/BJ92-S933)
7 W James (1897) *The Will to Believe, and Other Essays in Popular Philosophy*, Longmans, Green, and Co.
8 W James (1902) *The Varieties of Religious Experience: A study in human nature*, Longmans, Green, and Co.
9 A H Maslow (1954) *Motivation and Personality*, Harper & Row.
10 F Herzberg, B Mausner and B Bloch Snyderman (1959) *The Motivation to Work*, Wiley.
11 E L Deci and R M Ryan (1985) *Intrinsic Motivation and Self-Determination in Human Behavior*, Springer.
12 E L Deci and R M Ryan (1985) *Intrinsic Motivation and Self-Determination in Human Behavior*, Springer.
13 Deloitte. *2024 Gen Z and Millennial Survey: Living and working with purpose in a transforming world*, Deloitte, 2024. www.deloitte.com/global/en/issues/work/content/genz-millennialsurvey.html (archived at https://perma.cc/MR2D-7PTF)

14 G R Kellerman and M E P Seligman (2023) *Tomorrowmind: Thriving at work with resilience, creativity, and connection – now and in an uncertain future*, Atria Books.

15 D Kahneman (2011) *Thinking, Fast and Slow*, Farrar, Straus and Giroux.

16 B L Fredrickson and D Kahneman. Duration neglect in retrospective evaluations of affective episodes, *Journal of Personality and Social Psychology*, 1993, 65 (1), 45–55.

17 B Brown (2012) *Daring Greatly: How the courage to be vulnerable transforms the way we live, love, parent, and lead*, Gotham Books.

18 M Gielan (2015) *Broadcasting Happiness: The science of igniting and sustaining positive change*, BenBella Books.

19 E Seppälä (2016) *The Happiness Track: How to apply the science of happiness to accelerate your success*, HarperOne.

20 S Lyubomirsky (2008) *The How of Happiness: A new approach to getting the life you want*, Penguin Press.

21 L Santos and T Gendler. Knowing is not half the battle: The GI Joe fallacy, Interrobang, 2015, www.interrobang.is/2015/05/the-gi-joe-fallacy-knowing-is-not-half-the-battle (archived at https://perma.cc/BN5K-RUDH)

22 S Achor (2010) *The Happiness Advantage: How a positive brain fuels success in work and life*, Crown Business.

23 A Duckworth (2016) *Grit: The power of passion and perseverance*, Scribner.

24 T Ben-Shahar (2007) *Happier: Learn the secrets to daily joy and lasting fulfillment*, McGraw-Hill.

25 A Grant et al. Impact and the art of motivation maintenance: The effects of contact with beneficiaries on persistence behavior, *Organizational Behavior and Human Decision Processes*, 2007, 103 (1), 53–67.

26 A Grant (2023) *Hidden Potential: The science of achieving greater things*,Viking.

10

The future of happiness

We made it. Just so you know, my gratitude today will be for you sticking with me on this ride. I hope you've found the insights and research valuable. It's been incredible to look back at what I wrote ten years ago and see how much has changed and how much has stayed the same.

We've analysed happiness at work from a wide range of different perspectives and now we're nearing the end of that discussion. Before we conclude our time together, I want to use this final chapter to study the future of happiness. Over the next few pages we'll investigate what's on the horizon in the areas of research, policy, workplace shifts and scientific understanding.

In my talks I spend a considerable amount of time describing what's in store for happiness in the workplace and beyond. The amount of groundbreaking and truly exciting research may not be known commonly yet, but as we continue to evolve our curiosity and invest in our learning it's only a matter of time before we'll see happiness education take root inside our organizations and, inevitably, permanently inside our lives. My hope for you is that this final chapter will be a provocative and enlightening way to end an already entertaining topic.

Let's get into it.

Our future looks bright

Growing older may feel daunting in a youth-centred culture, but research shows that happiness often increases with age. Economist David Blanchflower's 2021 study of over 145 countries revealed a U-shaped happiness curve: high happiness in youth, a dip in midlife, then a steady rise into older age. Some researchers suggest that we're actually our happiest in our 70s.[1]

Blanchflower's research highlights that happiness isn't merely a product of youthful vitality but instead grows from mature emotional stability, perspective and acceptance. This change is supported by studies showing that older adults experience an increase in oxytocin release, fostering compassion and prosocial behaviours. The rise in oxytocin aligns with Blanchflower's theory: as people prioritize relationships and find satisfaction in low-key activities, they cultivate a happiness that resonates deeply in their later years.

Blanchflower himself, now in his 70s, exemplifies this shift. He finds joy in pastimes like fishing with his grandchildren, an experience he contrasts with his youthful pursuit of high-energy sports. His journey reflects his broader findings: that happiness in later life stems from adapting to one's evolving capacities and finding fulfilment in activities that align with those shifts. In other words, people often rediscover happiness when they stop chasing excitement and begin savouring life's quieter moments.[2]

If we're currently in that trough of despair – the mid-life – don't worry, happiness is just over the hill.

Humanizing technology

In the first edition of this book I wrote about Japanese scientists who'd already built a super-computer that mimics the brain cell network. To achieve this, they had to simulate a network consisting of 1.73 billion nerve cells connected by 10.4 trillion synapses. The process took 40 minutes to complete the simulation of one second of neuronal network activity in real, biological time.[3]

Since then, there have been incredible advancements in the tech. By 2020, scientists used the same computer to model an even larger brain network of 68 billion neurons. This simulation could even mimic certain brain-controlled tasks, like tracking moving objects with the eyes, showing that such models could become useful for studying brain function.

The latest progress, as of 2024, includes a new framework called CORTEX, built for Japan's Fugaku supercomputer. This framework speeds up large-scale brain simulations by handling synaptic connections more efficiently, making these simulations faster and closer to capturing real-time brain activity.[4]

These advances show that scientists are getting better at simulating brain functions, bringing us closer to understanding the brain on a larger scale and in more detail. These developments highlight the rapid progress in computational neuroscience, moving closer to real-time, large-scale simulations of the human brain.

In 2016 Gartner suggested that 6.4 billion connected things were in use worldwide.[5] In 2024 the integration of advanced technologies such as artificial neural networks, augmented reality (AR), and the Internet of Things (IoT) continued to reshape various sectors, including education, healthcare and commerce. The IoT landscape is experiencing rapid growth. By 2024 there were approximately 18.8 billion connected IoT devices worldwide, a number projected to more than double to 41.1 billion by 2030. This expansion underscores the increasing connectivity of physical objects embedded with technology, enabling seamless communication and interaction with their environments.[6]

With the proliferation of connected devices and immersive technologies, effective communication now requires greater emotional intelligence. The integration of AI and AR into daily interactions emphasizes the need for nuanced, empathetic engagement in both personal and professional contexts. This shift highlights the importance of developing deeper, more meaningful connections as technology becomes more intertwined with human experiences.

As this connectivity increases, communication with each other, our employees and our customers will require even more nuanced, emotional connection. Emotion AI, or affective computing, is rapidly evolving to make interactions with technology more emotionally intelligent. These systems can now detect human emotions through voice, facial expressions, text analysis and even physiological signals, such as heart rate or body language, allowing machines to respond in ways that feel more nuanced and empathetic.

A prime example of this is Hume AI, which has introduced an 'empathic voice interface'. Wired magazine describes how this technology enhances AI with emotionally expressive voices, allowing applications like customer service bots, personal assistants and even therapeutic tools to convey emotions such as compassion, warmth, or excitement. By simulating human-like emotional expressions, these interfaces aim to create a connection that feels more authentic and supportive. In contexts like telemedicine or online counselling, empathic voice interfaces can make interactions feel less robotic, offering a more comforting and personalized experience for users.[7]

Emotion AI is also being integrated into wellness applications. For instance, fitness and meditation apps use emotion detection to assess a user's emotional state, adapting guidance or offering mindfulness exercises based on stress levels or mood. Companies are exploring its use in education and healthcare, where it could help personalize learning experiences or provide patients with more emotionally aware responses, ultimately enhancing engagement and satisfaction.

AI's role in mental health care is also expanding significantly, offering new avenues for emotional support and therapy. Virtual AI companions, such as Woebot[8] and Replika[9] are designed to provide conversational support, helping users express their emotions, track mental health patterns, and even work through challenges with cognitive behavioural techniques. Some of these AI companions engage users in regular check-ins, prompting discussions about their feelings and offering scientifically backed strategies to manage stress and anxiety.

Interestingly, studies show that Gen Z and Millennials, who are more comfortable with digital interactions, are finding these AI companions beneficial. Some younger users feel more at ease sharing their emotions with AI, perceiving it as less judgemental than human interaction. In a *New York Post* article, a recent survey revealed that AI companions offer a sense of comfort and validation comparable to traditional emotional support animals, especially for those who may not have access to or feel ready for therapy.[10]

These AI companions are also appealing for their accessibility and affordability. Many are available on mobile devices and offer 24/7 support, allowing users to engage whenever they feel the need, even in the middle of the night. For individuals experiencing mild to moderate mental health concerns, these AI tools can be a helpful supplement to traditional therapy or a standalone support system. They provide users with a safe space to express feelings, build emotional resilience and learn coping strategies, bridging some gaps in mental health care access.

And, as we become more connected to each other and the Internet of Things, it appears that we are morphing into our technology. But, it also appears that technology is slowly morphing into us. With the rapid development of robots and the increasing humanization of their looks, their capabilities and behaviours, we're about to see a level of connection to our technology that only appeared in science fiction up until now.

When robots learn emotional intelligence

As robots become more advanced, their moral and ethical decision-making will only become more refined and complex. This provocative and growing debate has ethicists working hard to figure out a solution to a mind-bending question. Is it actually possible to programme ethics into robots and are we the species to do it? If yes, can we then trust 'them' to make moral decisions in an ongoing way?

Olivia Goldhill writing for Quartz says she sees two main approaches to creating an ethical robot. 'The first is to decide on a specific ethical law (maximize happiness, for example), write a code for such a law, and create a robot that strictly follows the code. But the difficulty here is deciding on the appropriate ethical rule. Every moral law, even the seemingly simple one above, has a myriad of exceptions and counter examples. For example, should a robot maximize happiness by harvesting the organs from one man to save five?'[11]

You see this same conundrum raised in the ethics of autonomous vehicles. If the car is forced to turn left and slam into an 8-year-old boy or turn right and strike an elderly woman, which direction should the vehicle choose?

This question of whether humans have the proper moral framework has only been vaguely decoded over the centuries we've had to ponder it, but here we are trying to figure it out and initialize it in robots after only barely skimming the surface of the implications. If we don't know the answers yet, then how can we make that programmatic in non-humans?

Another way to teach robots ethics could be through machine learning, where it can then respond in real time to ethical questions. To remove us as their teachers, Ronald Arkin, Professor and Director of the Mobile Robot Laboratory at Georgia Institute of Technology, is working on trying to make machines comply with international humanitarian law. 'In this case, there's a huge body of laws and instructions for machines to follow, which have been developed by humans and agreed by international states.'[12]

Wendall Wallach, co-author of the book *Moral Machines: Teaching robots right from wrong*, argues, 'Robot ethics can be seen as a problem of human ethics. Thinking about how robots ought to behave is a soul-searching exercise in how humans ought to behave.'[13]

Robot ethics, or 'roboethics', is a fascinating area that's all about figuring out the right way to create and use robots and AI. Recently, this field has seen some intriguing advancements that make you think about how these technologies fit into our world – and what kind of impact they'll have.

Meet Ai-Da, a humanoid robot that's shaking up the art world. Ai-Da uses cameras, AI algorithms and robotic arms to create original artwork. In October 2024 she made headlines when her abstract painting of Alan Turing, called 'AI God', was auctioned at Sotheby's. This wasn't just any art auction – this marked the first time a robot's artwork was sold at a major auction house. It's a moment that brings up some big questions: Who is the 'creator' here? What does it mean for AI to produce art, and what are the ethical implications of AI-generated creativity?[14]

When we think about robots entering our daily lives, it's essential that they interact with us fairly. Researchers are looking into how robots can be designed to avoid reinforcing social biases and to treat people equitably, regardless of background. This is an effort to ensure that as robots become more common, they don't accidentally carry forward the biases humans have – and that everyone, no matter who they are, can benefit from these advancements.

Whether we need them to connect with us on an ethical or moral level is an evolving discussion. We have to ask ourselves, why do robots have to express human-like emotions to improve our world? Do they actually require emotional intelligence and who is going to decide whether they should? Are we responsible for teaching them about happiness? What about sadness?

There are obviously many individuals who are concerned about the integration of robots into the workforce and what that might mean for the future of our happiness. One employee might say, 'I'm thrilled! I get some time back for my other duties. The new robot vacuum is tidying up the hotel floors while I make the beds.' Another employee could have the reverse reaction: 'I'm terrified. This is going to mean that I'm out of work. I used to vacuum the floors and now a robot is doing it for me.' These are the ethical and moral questions currently in our line of sight as leaders and yet there is so much grey area between the answers and us.

Vivian Giang wrote a provocative article for Fast Company titled 'Robots might take your job, but here's why you shouldn't worry'. She claims that the proliferation of robots won't actually mean that everyone is about to be unemployed. Although she agrees that it's easy to see why we might have cause to worry.[15]

The Henn-na Hotel in Japan is the world's first hotel to be 90 per cent staffed by humanoid robots. The robots, called 'actroids', manufactured by robot maker Kokoro, will be responsible for greeting and checking in guests, all the while establishing eye contact and responding to body language.[16]

The futuristic robots have been designed to look as though they are breathing and have eyes that blink. The Henn-na Hotel, which means 'strange hotel' in English, use the actroids along with other robots, including Aldebaran Robotics' NAO humanoid robot and SoftBank's Pepper humanoid robot to make up its staff of three receptionist robots, four service and porter robots, an industrial robot responsible for guests' coats and bags and several cleaning robots.

According to their website, the humanoid robots are multi-lingual, able to converse with guests in Japanese, English, Korean and Chinese. Robots will deliver room service, which can be ordered via a tablet.

Although some human staff will be on hand to ensure service is not compromised, robots will maintain all the housekeeping. They will also carry luggage and greet guests at reception. Doors are fitted with facial recognition technology so guests can access rooms without the need for key cards. And, room temperature is controlled by a system that detects the body heat of guests and adjusts accordingly.

Giang describes how other hotel chains are getting into the robot mix. For example, the giant hotel chain Starwood introduced its robotics staff called Botlrs, responsible for delivering niceties to guests by navigating around hotels and using elevators without any humans to help them.

Nine years ago for the first edition, I wrote that Amazon were just developing their drone shipping programme and had up to 15,000 robots in their warehouses to keep up with customers' orders. By 2024 they were deploying 750,000 robots across their warehouses.

I also wrote that hospitals were using robots to deliver trays of food and drugs, clean linens and take out the trash. By 2024 robots were changing the face of healthcare. Here are five game-changing examples according to Case Western Reserve University:

1 The da Vinci® Surgical Robot is a multi-armed wonderbot, being used to reduce surgical errors and make surgery less invasive for thousands of patients.

2 The Xenex is an automated and portable robot used to disinfect entire hospital rooms in minutes using pulsed, full-spectrum UV rays that kill a range of infectious bacteria – even as risky as Methicillin-resistant Staphylococcus aureus (MRSA).

3 The PARO Therapeutic Robot is an interactive device that looks like a baby harbour seal and is designed to provide the benefits of animal

therapy without relying on live animals. PARO is used extensively with elderly patients with dementia, and has been proven to reduce stress and provide comfort to anxious patients. The fuzzy PARO can respond to its name, enjoys being stroked, and, over time, develops a customized, pleasing personality tailored by its memory of previous interactions.

4 The CyberKnife is a robotic surgery system that delivers radiation therapy to tumours with sub-millimetre precision. It allows for treatment of tumours in areas of the body that were once surgically complex to operate on, including the prostate, head, neck and liver. It's non-invasive and minimizes the exposure of healthy organs and tissues to radiation.

5 TUG is an autonomous mobile robot used to ferry supplies to where they are needed, freeing employees from heavy physical loads and allowing them to focus on patient care. One estimate shows that a typical 200-bed hospital moves meals, linens, lab samples, waste and other items the equivalent of 53 miles per day.[17]

I also wrote about how home-improvement chain Lowe's deployed a robot greeter that shows customers where items are throughout the store. Today, those robots have been turned into 400-pound robo-security that patrol parking lots and stores to protect from theft.[18]

As a happiness advocate, I feel like something went wrong.

At the time, Giang shared that even the US Army is reportedly considering replacing tens of thousands of soldiers with robots. It has yet to happen officially, but progress has been made. Retired US General Milley told Axios that he expects about a third of the military will be made up of robot soldiers in due time.[19]

As these technologies progress, governments and organizations are working to keep up by establishing rules and policies to guide the ethical use of robots and AI. These frameworks aim to strike a balance: pushing for innovation while ensuring these technologies are used responsibly and with societal well-being in mind. With rapid developments, having guidelines in place helps make sure we're moving forward thoughtfully.

Overall, robot ethics is shaping up to be a critical field that goes beyond just tech – it's about how these creations fit into our values, how they reflect (or don't reflect) us, and how they impact our future. It's a space where everyone from researchers to policymakers is joining in the conversation, ensuring we're prepared for the ethical twists and turns ahead.

How will this change the workforce?

In 2013, Carl Benedikt Frey and Michael Osborne examined the impact of technology on employment in their paper 'The future of employment: How susceptible are jobs to computerisation?' They analysed 702 detailed occupations and, based on their research, they estimated about 47 per cent of total US employment is at risk. Their paper was motivated by John Maynard Keynes' prediction of widespread technological unemployment.[20]

The paper references Brynjolfsson and McAfee, who in 2012 wrote that 'the pace of technological innovation is still increasing, but with more sophisticated software technologies disrupting labour markets by making workers redundant'.[21] The authors note that routine manufacturing tasks aren't the only examples where computerization is taking over jobs. The autonomous driverless car provides one example of how manual tasks in transport and logistics would soon be automated.

However, a study by MIT provides evidence that innovations augmenting human labour tend to create new work, whereas those automating tasks may slow job creation. The research highlights the importance of focusing on technologies that enhance human capabilities rather than replace them.

These recent analyses underscore a nuanced view of AI and automation's impact on employment. While certain jobs are at risk of displacement, there is also significant potential for job creation in emerging sectors. The emphasis is on adapting to technological changes through skill development and focusing on roles that leverage human creativity and emotional intelligence.

However, if we examine the pace of innovation, it's no surprise that we're constantly creating brand new jobs. And not just new jobs in existing industries, but at an unparalleled pace we're also watching new jobs forming in new fields that never existed until now. Who would have expected that making robots look like humans and teaching AI to get better at telling a joke would be responsible for thousands of jobs – but here we are.

Adding 'smartness' for organizations will force us to make decisions as leaders about how integrated we want our employees to be. We've already witnessed large organizations imbed sensors in items worn by their employees to allow connectivity with the rest of their devices. This allows for projects to move from room to room, capable of uploading on smart boards in every meeting room. And not just from room to room inside a specific building, but throughout the various countries in which they do business.

As we've discussed, this kind of tracking has proven to be problematic, but is there ever a use case for how it might be beneficial? I believe it's all based on what kind of cultures we're building. If these technologies are used specifically for their purpose and not for micromanaging they can be helpful.

I think it's great that I can take my presentation with me on my wearable device as I travel for speaking events in remote parts of the world. This kind of simplicity is exactly what I am longing for. However, we are still a long way from having a single vision that would make everyone feel happy about our interconnection between work, technology and each other.

Can it get any faster?

Today, approximately 347.3 billion emails are sent daily worldwide. This translates to about 240 million emails per minute. The pace of work is intense. And, that's on top of our adoption of new technology generally. Figure 10.1 demonstrates how the speed of adoption has accelerated exponentially.

FIGURE 10.1 Time taken to reach 100 million users across various platforms

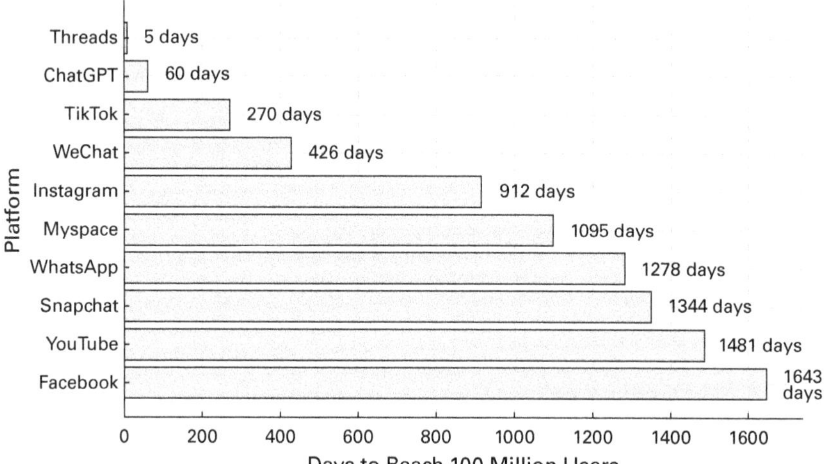

As technology starts to close in on us, David Cox, Chief Medical Officer of Headspace, believes that by 2030 employers will work towards building a more mindful work environment that promotes technology-free days and redesigned workspaces to allow both open-plan collaborative spaces and secluded workstations that support daydreaming.

Mindfulness is also being explored through new technology and exploratory techniques in brain science. With new experiments being initiated in the field of neurosciences, we may be able to truly understand what mindfulness means. New science should tell us how much quiet and calm is required to become happier and healthier in an increasingly stressed-out world.

Researchers at the University of Arizona have utilized low-intensity transcranial-focused ultrasound (tFUS) to non-invasively target the brain's default mode network, particularly the posterior cingulate cortex. This area is associated with activities like daydreaming and self-referential thinking. By modulating this region, tFUS has been shown to reduce mind-wandering and enhance mindfulness, offering a novel approach to improving present-moment awareness.[22]

Companies are also developing wearable devices that monitor brain activity to enhance focus and mindfulness. For instance, Neurable's MW75 Neuro headphones use electroencephalography (EEG) sensors to track attention levels, providing real-time feedback to help users maintain concentration and manage mental fatigue. Such technologies aim to integrate mindfulness practices into daily routines through biofeedback mechanisms.[23]

It makes sense that employers are seeking new ways to reduce distractibility and increase focus for their employees. With so much noise coming at us from our technology, leveraging mindfulness and meditation are valuable skills.

A large body of research has established the efficacy of these mindfulness-based interventions in reducing symptoms of a number of disorders, including anxiety,[24] depression,[25] substance abuse,[26] eating disorders[27] and chronic pain, [28] as well as improving well-being and quality of life.[29]

A 2015 study demonstrated that significant increases in the density of grey matter occurred with meditation. Since that early study, neuroscientists have looked deeper into the impacts of mediation on the structure of the brain.[30]

One area of the brain, found deep inside the forebrain behind the frontal lobe, happens to be associated with self-regulation, directed attention and behaviour. It is responsible for your 'edit' switch, so you don't blurt out awkward comments, and it can help you manage impulsivity and unchecked aggression.

In the 2015 article 'Mindfulness can literally change your brain', authors Christina Congleton, Britta Hölzel and Sara Lazar describe how those with impaired connections between the frontal lobe and other brain regions perform poorly on tests of mental flexibility: they hold on to ineffective problem-solving strategies rather than adapting their behaviour. Meditators, on the other hand, demonstrate superior performance on tests of self-regulation, resisting distractions and making correct answers more often than non-meditators. This area of the brain is also associated with learning from past experience to support optimal decision-making.[31]

Another area of the brain that meditation can positively alter is the hippocampus region. This is a seahorse-shaped area buried inside the temple on each side of the brain and is part of the limbic system, a set of inner structures associated with emotion and memory.

It is covered in receptors for the stress hormone cortisol, and studies have shown that it can be damaged by chronic stress, contributing to a harmful spiral in the body. Indeed, people with stress-related disorders like depression and PTSD tend to have a smaller hippocampus.

When we meditate we increase our dopamine and other healthy hormones that can act as a prophylactic measure to the harm that comes with the stress hormone cortisol. Neuroscientists have also shown that practising mindfulness affects brain areas related to perception, body awareness, pain tolerance, emotion regulation, introspection, complex thinking and sense of self.[32]

Mindfulness will no longer be just a recommendation in the future of our workplaces; it will be a necessity to lead with mindfulness. To ensure higher levels of self-regulation and effective decision-making capabilities, and to protect ourselves from toxic stress, we will need to be the 'poster child' for healthiness inside our organizations. This is actually becoming a common well-being practice for some companies today.

Take Lululemon, for example – they offer meditation classes throughout the workday so employees can take time to regroup, centre their thoughts and come back to the rest of their day refreshed and ready to innovate and create.

Maybe this would be a good time to see what kind of spaces you have available in your office to include mindfulness as part of your employee well-being experience.

Frankenstein, or just great science?

Perhaps it's a retinal chip that will allow you to see in the dark, or a cochlear implant that lets you hear any conversation in a noisy restaurant, no matter how loud. Or a memory chip, wired directly into your brain's hippocampus, that gives you perfect recall of everything you read. Or, an implanted interface with the internet that automatically translates a clearly articulated silent thought into an online search that digested the relevant webpage and projected a summary directly into your brain.

Gary Marcus and Christof Koch investigated these questions about brain implants and other incredible science that is right on the cusp of making its way into our lives today. Certainly we'll see these innovations come to reality in the next decade, but for now it still sounds a little like science fiction.

In 2014, Marcus and Koch wrote in 'The future of brain implants' for the *Wall Street Journal* that 'brain implants today are where laser eye surgery was several decades ago. They are not risk-free and make sense only for a narrowly defined set of patients – but they are a sign of things to come'.[33] Just like pacemakers, dental crowns or implantable insulin pumps seemed to be the wave of the future not that long ago, neuroprosthetics will be the way we 'restore or supplement the mind's capacities with electronics inserted directly into the nervous system [and it will] change how we perceive the world and move through it. For better or worse, these devices become part of who we are'.

A now-common implant is already used by thousands of Parkinson's patients around the world. This neuroprosthetic device sends electrical pulses deep into the brain and activates some of the pathways involved in motor control. Although it doesn't cure the disease, it helps to reduce (and even eliminate in some cases) the tremors and rigidity symptomatic of Parkinson's.

And, what about our desire to increase effectiveness and speed? In one study, electrical stimulation to the brain during a video game session increased players' speed and accuracy.[34]

Eventually, neural implants will go from handling life or death situations to 'enhancing the performance of healthy or "normal" people', say Marcus and Koch. 'They will be used to improve memory, mental focus (Ritalin without the side effects), perception and mood.'

Some of the more radical advancements today include technologies that could allow for the precise editing of memories or the modification of emotional responses. Leveraging advancements in CRISPR gene-editing and neurogenomics, future tools might offer treatments for trauma or PTSD by 'rewriting' traumatic memories or altering the neural pathways associated with certain emotions, offering a new realm of mental health interventions.[35]

Research in brain-to-brain communication is gaining traction, and by 2040 we may see systems enabling direct, non-verbal communication between people. This could create 'neural links' that transmit thoughts, feelings or complex concepts directly, bypassing language. Imagine applications in therapy where therapists can experience a client's emotions directly, creating a new level of empathy.[36]

In the future, it's predicted that AI will help create 'digital twins' of individuals' brains, mapping consciousness with exceptional accuracy. These digital twins could simulate a person's mental health conditions, allowing researchers to experiment with potential treatments on the twin before real-world application. This would be revolutionary for personalized mental health care, offering a virtual space to test interventions and predict responses.[37]

Neuroadaptive architecture aims to create spaces that respond to occupants' mental states. By 2040, offices, homes and even public spaces may use biofeedback and brainwave sensors to adjust lighting, temperature or sound based on mood or stress levels. Imagine an office space that senses when someone is feeling anxious and adjusts to a calming environment, or a home that energizes when it senses fatigue.

Advances in synthetic biology and nanotechnology may lead to the development of synthetic synapses that can replace or repair damaged brain regions. This could revolutionize treatment for mental health conditions that stem from neural dysfunction, such as severe depression or schizophrenia, by 'patching' parts of the brain that are not functioning properly.[38]

Implantable devices might be designed to deliver real-time stress relief by stimulating areas associated with relaxation and focus. Think of it as a 'neuro-pacemaker' for stress or perhaps a 'neuro-*peace*maker' is a more apt term. When it detects elevated stress levels, it activates brain circuits to restore calm and focus, helping users remain grounded in the present moment.[39]

These predictions reflect a deeper integration between neuroscience and advanced technology, pushing beyond what we see today. If realized, they would fundamentally reshape how we approach mental health, wellness and human connection, offering tools that sound like science fiction but are actively being researched.

As always – with radical innovations comes radical moral dilemmas. What if those implants get hacked? If our employer supplies the tech, does it belong to them? What about the data? Or are neuronal implants a case of 'bring your own device' to work?

Some futurists believe that within the next twenty years we'll be wired directly into the cloud, from brain to toe. But, as we advance into this unknown territory, we'll need to keep asking ourselves, 'Are we making the right decisions?'

From robots that make life a little bit smoother, to technology taking over our jobs, to transplanting happier thoughts into our brains, the future is going to be undeniably complex and thrilling and surprising. Will this extreme connectivity make us happier, more tied to our communities and to the human race at large? Will it make us more productive and have a life with more meaning? Or will it separate us? Will some of us have super powers and the rest of us remain 'unenhanced'? Will progress mean salvation, or destruction?

This is both the exciting aspect and the terrifying part about the future. We can imagine, but we can't predict.

What I am absolutely certain of, however, is that the future is closer than we think. And, we'll never run out of topics to debate about what new 'thing' is helping or hindering our happiness. From Socrates to today, we're still questioning which predictions to ignore, which ones to vehemently deny and which ones to embrace wholeheartedly. If we can learn anything from history, some of the innovations and philosophies we questioned the most, the ones we were most afraid of, the ones that seemed the most impossible, somehow found their way into our world.

So, before I leave you, my question is this – what do you predict? Will we move closer to a world of well-being and of belonging? Will we fight for our humanity – our community – a return to the village?

I hope so.

I am longing for a return to happiness. The choices we make as individuals becomes the choice of the choosing happiness through kindness towards others. And don't we want this happiness 'thing', despite its arguable flaws and its intangibility and unpredictability, to find its way back into our world? I would argue that we've never needed it more.

Notes

1. D Blanchflower. Is happiness U-shaped everywhere? Age and subjective wellbeing in 145 countries. *Journal of Population Economics*, 2021, 34, 575–624. doi.org/10.1007/s00148-020-00797-z (archived at https://perma.cc/N8P3-NXK4)
2. D Blanchflower. Is happiness U-shaped everywhere? Age and subjective well-being in 145 countries. *Jurnal of Population Economics*, 2021, 34,

575–624. doi.org/10.1007/s00148-020-00797-z (archived at https://perma.cc/N8P3-NXK4)

3 M van Rijmenam. How unlimited computing power, swarms of sensors and algorithms will rock our world, Datafloq, 2016. datafloq.com/read/unlimited-computing-swarm-sensors-algorithms-world (archived at https://perma.cc/YSH9-3KSJ)

4 T Lyu, et al. CORTEX: Large-scale brain simulator utilizing indegree sub-graph decomposition on Fugaku supercomputer, arXiv, 2024. arxiv.org/abs/2406.03762 (archived at https://perma.cc/48KY-J5AA)

5 IOT Business News. Gartner says 6.4 billion connected 'things' will be in use in 2016, up 30 percent from 2015, IoT Business News, 2015. iotbusinessnews.com/2015/11/10/46231-gartner-says-6-4-billion-connected-things-will-be-in-use-in-2016-up-30-percent-from-2015 (archived at https://perma.cc/MQA7-9ADN)

6 Exploding Topics. 60+ amazing IoT statistics (2024-2030), Exploding Topics, 2024. explodingtopics.com/blog/iot-stats (archived at https://perma.cc/TS4C-U54X)

7 W Knight. This new tech puts AI in touch with its emotions – and yours, *Wired*, 2024. www.wired.com/story/hume-ai-emotional-intelligence (archived at https://perma.cc/E5ZA-7BJW)

8 A Ohnouna. Woebot: The robo-therapist supplying comfort, consolation, and care at scale, Harvard Business School Digital Initiative, 2023. d3.harvard.edu/platform-digit/submission/woebot-the-robo-therapist-supplying-comfort-consolation-and-care-at-scale (archived at https://perma.cc/PPN9-47BJ)

9 S Shah. Replika: AI similar to Replika, Yeti AI, nd. yetiai.com/ai-similar-to-replika (archived at https://perma.cc/J62J-BZKR)

10 A Grace. Gen Zs, millennials are using AI for emotional support, calling it 'more effective' than a pet: Study, *New York Post*, 2024. nypost.com/2024/10/09/lifestyle/gen-z-millennials-more-comforted-by-ai-over-emotional-support-pets (archived at https://perma.cc/672J-N3WC)

11 O Goldhill. Can we trust robots to make moral decisions? Quartz, 2016. qz.com/653575/can-we-trust-robots-to-make-moral-decisions (archived at https://perma.cc/6B6J-5XGT)

12 ICRC. *Autonomous Weapon Systems: Technical, military, legal and humanitarian aspects*, International Committee of the Red Cross, 2014. www.icrc.org/sites/default/files/document/file_list/4221-002-autonomous-weapons-systems-full-report.pdf (archived at https://perma.cc/X2R6-97BU)

13 W Wallach and C Allen (2009) *Moral Machines: Teaching robots right from wrong*, Oxford University Press.

14 A Diaz. First art piece painted by humanoid robot sells at auction for a whopping $1 million, *New York Post*, 2024. nypost.com/2024/11/08/lifestyle/

first-art-piece-painted-by-humanoid-robot-sells-at-auction-for-a-whopping-1-million/ (archived at https://perma.cc/3MZB-JUX6).

15 V Giang. Robots might take your job, but here's why you shouldn't worry, Fast Company, 2015. www.fastcompany.com/3049079/robots-might-take-your-job-but-heres-why-you-shouldnt-worry (archived at https://perma.cc/RLT3-X5GW)

16 CBS News. A night in Japan's robot hotel, CBS News, 2015. www.cbsnews.com/news/inside-japan-robot-hotel-hennna-where-staff-are-robots (archived at https://perma.cc/NG29-6VZA)

17 Case Western Reserve University. Medical Robots Making a Difference, Case Western Reserve University, nd. online-engineering.case.edu/blog/medical-robots-making-a-difference (archived at https://perma.cc/2EJW-NWNC)

18 B Tobin. Lowe's is testing autonomous robots shaped like eggs to patrol parking lots and deter crime, Business Insider, 2023. www.businessinsider.com/lowes-tests-egg-shaped-autonomous-robots-patrol-lots-theft-crime-2023-3 (archived at https://perma.cc/9GAH-MV7N)

19 R Ceder. One-third of US military could be robotic by 2039, Milley says, Military Times, 2024. www.militarytimes.com/news/2024/07/14/one-third-of-us-military-could-be-robotic-by-2039-milley (archived at https://perma.cc/8CFL-QAZE)

20 C B Frey and M A Osborne. The future of employment: How susceptible are jobs to computerisation? Future of Humanity Institute, 2013. www.fhi.ox.ac.uk/wp-content/uploads/The-Future-of-Employment-How-Susceptible-Are-Jobs-to-Computerization.pdf (archived at https://perma.cc/XAD9-R95U)

21 E Brynjolfsson and A McAfee. *Race Against the Machine*, MIT Center for Digital Business, 2012. https://ide.mit.edu/sites/default/files/publications/Brynjolfsson_McAfee_Race_Against_the_Machine.pdf (archived at https://perma.cc/X9DR-JXQQ)

22 T Zhang et al. Transcranial focused ultrasound (tFUS) and neuromodulation, *Frontiers in Human Neuroscience*, 2021. www.frontiersin.org/journals/human-neuroscience/articles/10.3389/fnhum.2021.749162/full (archived at https://perma.cc/5AJ8-QL5B)

23 E Mullin. I tried these brain-tracking headphones that claim to improve focus, Wired, 2024. www.wired.com/story/this-brain-tracking-device-wants-to-help-you-work-smarter (archived at https://perma.cc/W5RM-Q8L6)

24 L Roemer, S Orsillo and K Salters-Pedneault. Efficacy of an acceptance-based behaviour therapy for generalized anxiety disorder: Evaluation in a randomized controlled trial, *Journal of Consulting and Clinical Psychology*, 2003, 76, 1083–89.

25 J Teasdale, et al. Prevention of relapse/recurrence in major depression by mindfulness-based cognitive therapy, *Journal of Consulting and Clinical Psychology*, 2000, 68, 615–23.

26 S Bowen, et al. Mindfulness meditation and substance use in an incarcerated population, *Psychology of Addictive Behaviours*, 2006, pp 343–47.

27 K Tapper et al. Exploratory randomised controlled trial of a mindfulness-based weight loss intervention for women, *Appetite*, 2009, 52, 396–404.

28 P Grossman, et al. Mindfulness training as an intervention for fibromyalgia: Evidence of postintervention and 3-year follow-up benefits in well-being, *Psychotherapy and Psychosomatics*, 2007, 76, 226–33.

29 J Carmody and R Baer. Relationships between mindfulness practice and levels of mindfulness, medical and psychological symptoms and well-being in a mindfulness-based stress reduction program, *Journal of Behavioral Medicine*, 2008, 31, 23–33.

30 C Congleton, W Holzel and S Lazar. Mindfulness can literally change your brain, *Harvard Business Review*, 2015. hbr.org/2015/01/mindfulness-can-literally-change-your-brain (archived at https://perma.cc/4M86-QZ2U)

31 C Congleton, W Holzel and S Lazar. Mindfulness can literally change your brain, *Harvard Business Review*, 2015. hbr.org/2015/01/mindfulness-can-literally-change-your-brain (archived at https://perma.cc/4M86-QZ2U)

32 B Hölzel, Y Tang and M Posner. The neuroscience of mindfulness meditation, *Nature Reviews Neuroscience*, 2015, 16, 213–25.

33 G Marcus and C Koch. The future of brain implants, *The Wall Street Journal*, 2014. www.wsj.com/articles/SB100014240527023049149045794355929817805 28 (archived at https://perma.cc/86FK-7CEE)

34 C Y Looi et al. Combining brain stimulation and video game to promote long-term transfer of learning and cognitive enhancement, *Scientific Reports*, 2016, 6, 22003. www.nature.com/articles/srep22003.pdf (archived at https://perma.cc/HQF9-GPWF)

35 S Reardon. 'Treasure trove' of new CRISPR systems holds promise for genome editing, *Nature*, 2023. www.nature.com/articles/d41586-023-03697-w (archived at https://perma.cc/4U5S-BPGN)

36 D Armstrong and M Ma. Researcher controls colleague's motions in 1st human brain-to-brain interface, University of Washington, 2013. www.washington.edu/news/2013/08/27/researcher-controls-colleagues-motions-in-1st-human-brain-to-brain-interface (archived at https://perma.cc/GEJ4-UH4Z)

37 Y Jiang, et al. BrainNet: A multi-person brain-to-brain interface for direct collaboration between brains, arXiv, 2018. arxiv.org/abs/1809.08632 (archived at https://perma.cc/4RYK-S42V)

38 S Kunimichi, et al. A synthetic synaptic organizer protein restores glutamatergic neuronal circuits, *Science*, 2020. www.science.org/doi/10.1126/science.abb4853 (archived at https://perma.cc/92BS-8RVG)

39 Cleveland Clinic. Deep brain stimulation (DBS), Cleveland Clinic, nd. my.clevelandclinic.org/health/treatments/21088-deep-brain-stimulation (archived at https://perma.cc/R7MU-RZWV)

Conclusion

I love the wisdom of great minds and wish I were better at recalling their words. I also happen to be embarrassingly bad at telling jokes. Ask my husband Jim about this one and he'll laugh and agree. My jokes make others feel mostly awkward, empathetic and confused. I weave a pretty decent story, but those one-liners – just not my thing.

But, there is this one guy. You may know him. He goes by the name of Leo. Not Leo DiCaprio (although he's a pretty talented guy too) but the guy I'm talking about is Leo Tolstoy. Although you wouldn't peg him as an icon of happiness, this is why I'm mad about him. From *War and Peace* to *Anna Karenina*, Tolstoy liked to talk about how happiness and unhappiness, just like love and morality, are a choice. This encapsulates happiness for me. It also emphasizes how everything is a choice. From our flossing habits to our marriage vows to our leadership promises.

Leo has a one-liner that I will never bungle. I commissioned the artist Lisa Attygalle to create a painting that imagined my third child Lyla before I'd even met her – before she'd even entered this strange and wonderful planet. When I brought the painting home, I wept: her tiny figure was staring back at me from the painting on the wall. Although Lyla was still imaginary, still cocooned in my belly, I felt like I already knew her intimately.

In this moment there she was: sitting in a dramatic green field, under a blue sky filled with puffy white clouds. I knew this one sentence would be forever attached to my feelings for this imaginary blonde, blue-eyed child. The one that might have never been. Leo said this and I now give it to you: 'If you want to be happy, be.'

I find it necessary to go back to these aspects of my life that have defined my leadership. As Raj Sisodia stated, leaders have 'aha' moments that change them and turn them on to a path focused on bettering the world. These moments have altered me permanently too. For me, it began as I developed my lifelong friends, graduated university, when I became a wife, then a parent and I had others in my life to care for, to be better for, to be stronger for and to dream harder for.

When I went to work after having my first child, I suddenly realized that I was giving up so much to be there. My first instinct was to make it count. This incredible child was waiting for me at home to teach her how to say her first words, to be smothered in smiling kisses and to give her the confidence to be a woman. No longer would I wish away my days waiting for something more exciting, or long for an engaging project to fall on my lap, or complain that I wasn't getting enough out of my work. I was going to start making choices about my experiences. I could make my work worthwhile, or I could make it a waste of my time. If I wasn't going to feel enthusiastic about my job, or find the healthy positives in it, then why show up?

When Olivia was born, she came at a time of chaos and turbulence. My husband was unwell, and I felt very much alone. Liv came in to fill that empty space of fear and to help me believe that I could keep moving forward. She would offer me peace to make those big decisions, like moving back to Canada and starting a new chapter. Every one of my children has offered me a new insight, a window into who I am as a person and how I want to lead.

But, this catalyst moment is very different from one individual to another. It doesn't require becoming a parent to be hit hard with a life-changing pivot. Some would say that they had a spiritual realization. Others, it was a moment of clarity about their own mortality. For others, they suddenly understood what it meant to have excess and wanted to break down the barriers between them and the rest of the world. For some, it can simply be explained as an intrinsic desire to lead a purpose-driven life both at home and at work. For me, it was and still is unconditional love.

This book commits to the topic of unlocking happiness at work and I am emphatic that it's not just good for our souls, but good for business too. We need to focus our strategies on building happier individuals in the workplace, not just because it makes sound business sense, but also because it's the right thing to do. However, by now, after all the science and case studies and research and data, we've arrived at a juncture. This is where it all boils down to one singular decision point, and that's you.

What I am trying to get at here is that there comes a time when we choose a path of moral good and we choose caring over inconsideration. If you authentically want to make a difference in the lives of others, do. If you truly want to lead with compassion, then do.

I am so entirely grateful for the time you've spent with me over the pages of this book. I hope I've helped in some small way to spark your own internal dialogue on the topic and initiated some external conversations as well. As you continue to explore what this means for you and your role as leader, try to always keep in mind that life is about the choices we make. And kindness is a choice worth making.

In other words, if you want to be happy, be.

ACKNOWLEDGEMENTS

'Silent gratitude isn't very much use to anyone.'

GERTRUDE STEIN

As kindness became a key theme for the second edition of this book, I return to it here in the acknowledgements. If it weren't for the kindness shown to me each and every day – the people I am honoured to call my family and friends – we wouldn't be here having this conversation.

I am grateful for all of you. I have culled my thankyou's from the first edition but you are more than welcome to seek them out for a good read. I decided to wrap it all up a bit quicker, in my final act of kindness while writing this book.

Gratitude 1

Thank you, Jim. I want you to know that your mission to give so many lives a new perspective has changed my line of sight in a profound and positive way. I am forever grateful for you and your ability to persevere, your sacrifice and your love. I also want to thank you for continuing to learn – in all ways – with me, for me and for yourself. Your brain suits you.

Gratitude 2

Thank you, Willow, Liv and Lyla. Thank you for teaching me resilience and fortitude and silliness, and how to be funny and true to myself. I can say with authority that if you hadn't been so filled with unshakeable confidence in me, I wouldn't have made it to the end of this process. Thank you for being interesting and insightful and observant. I love you. I am in love with you. You are all magic.

Gratitude 3

Thank you, family. Mom and dad, thank you for your unwavering faith in me and passing down your hopefulness and optimism. It keeps this work very real to me as I strive each day to walk the talk. I don't think you can even guess how much love I have for you both.

To my siblings; Janice, my sister, 'Aunty' and the best cheerleader a person could have in their life. Thank you, Allen, for listening and engaging with my passion for talking social justice and trying to fix the world. Thank you, Melissa, for talking shop and acting as a sounding board and for always jumping in with help. My sister and brother-in-law, Patti and Steve, thank you for role modelling strength. Your bravery and perseverance is extraordinary – you continue to rise and show love and kindness in the face of great adversity.

To my mother and father-in-law, Connie and Ron, for your love and pride. I lucked out. You continue to be my champions and friends.

Gratitude 4

Thank you, friends. Thank you, Lydia for being my person. There is no other like you. I see inside your brain and you see into mine. We are soulmates. Thank you to my people, Michelle Venerus, Jen Schneider and Jen Wiens – you are so much of a great thing and it's never too much. You get me. You accept me. You make me feel safe.

Thank you, editors. Thank you, Chris Cudmore, for your enthusiasm for the second edition and making this update happen. It's been such a trip to rediscover what I wrote a decade ago. Thanks to the cat distribution system – I believe it may have been responsible for putting Chris and I on this path to rethinking happiness in the post-pandemic era of work.

Gratitude 5

Thank you, book. Thank you for reminding me why I put that note in our school's grade six time capsule to my future self. I wrote, 'Congratulations for receiving the John Newbery Medal, for the most distinguished contribution to children's literature.'

I was certain I would be a published writer one day. I guess the idea of non-fiction would have seemed boring then – but the goal remained. Although the Newbery Award remains elusive (could be forever since I don't write children's books), I feel like I succeeded.

Unlocking Happiness at Work was my first book and a major milestone. It's great to be here ten years later writing a second edition. What a humbling and happy moment – I am forever grateful that I get to live out my dream.

It's not easy. Writing is a love. A relationship that is both deeply satisfying and painfully tedious. It's how I wish I could speak – copy-edited and fact-checked, vulnerable yet sure on my feet. *UHAW*, thanks for being my first.

Thank you, reader. Books are vulnerable and so are authors these days so thank you for spending your hard-earned money to get into this discussion with me. I hope it was valuable and that you continue our conversation. It's worth having. Life is short. Let's strive to spend those 90,000 hours at work feeling more joy, having more fun and experiencing a lot more happiness.

INDEX

Also from Kogan Page

Why the happiest workplaces are the most successful

Mark Price

ISBN: 9781398617360

www.koganpage.com

EU Representative (GPSR)

Authorised Rep Compliance Ltd, Ground Floor, 71 Lower Baggot Street, Dublin, D02 P593, Ireland

www.arccompliance.com

www.ingramcontent.com/pod-product-compliance
Lightning Source LLC
Chambersburg PA
CBHW052356030425
24599CB00018B/562

* 9 7 8 1 3 9 8 6 1 9 4 6 3 *